RADIANT PEACE®
Wisdom & Tips from Children

Compiled by Ann Healy
Executive Director
The Radiant Peace Foundation International, Inc.

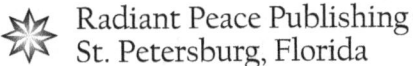

Radiant Peace Publishing
St. Petersburg, Florida

Copyright ©2013
The Radiant Peace Foundation International, Inc.

Published by Radiant Peace Publishing
P.O. Box 40822, St. Petersburg FL 33743

*All proceeds from the sale of this book benefit
The Radiant Peace Foundation International, Inc.*

Cover design & typography by Shoshana Shay

Radiant Peace® and The Radiant Peace Education Awards® are registered service marks held by The Radiant Peace Foundation International, Inc.

Publisher's Cataloging-in-Publication Data
Radiant Peace : wisdom & tips from children / compiled by Ann Healy.
   p. ; cm.
   Summary: A collection of award-winning essays and quotes selected from the first twenty-two years of The Radiant Peace Education Awards program.
   ISBN: 978-0-9892214-0-5

   1. Conduct of life–Literary collections. 2. Conduct of life–Quotations, maxims, etc. 3. Children's writings–Awards. 4. Essays. 5. Quotations. 6. Children's writings. I. Healy, Ann, 1952- II. The Radiant Peace Foundation International. III. Title: Wisdom & tips from children

PN6071.C697 R34 2013
810.8/02/06   2013911973

Service Marks Usage

Table of Contents

Acknowledgement

This book would not have been possible without Dr. Barbara Ray, Ph.D., Founder of The Radiant Peace Foundation International, Inc. and The International Museum of Radiant Peace. It was Dr. Ray's concept to begin an educational program to award children for their written expressions of Radiant Peace®. In 1990 this idea became The Radiant Peace Education Awards® program. Every essay in this book, along with thousands of others not yet published, is a result of this unique program.

Dr. Ray is a life-long educator. Her many accomplishments have given vision and breadth to the Foundation's programs. Dr. Ray is a retired professor of Classics (Latin and Greek), has a Ph.D. in Humanities with majors in Latin, Greek, Renaissance Art History and Modern Art History from Florida State University, and attained a Fulbright scholarship in Art History in Italy. She is a member of Phi Beta Kappa and Mensa and has traveled throughout the world. As a result of Dr. Ray's commitment to Radiant Peace this book now exists and is opening a gateway for you, the reader, to learn about Radiant Peace.

Preface

I n 1992, I first learned about The Radiant Peace Education Awards®. At that time I was a library media specialist at an elementary school in Alabama. The postmark deadline for submitting entries was fast approaching and I encouraged a small group of students to participate. Little did I know that twenty-one years later I would be compiling this book of essays! For many years after that first experience, hundreds of students from this school participated annually. When I searched the archives preparing this book, I came across many of the names of those students.

A few years later, I volunteered to be part of a team evaluating essays received from schools throughout the United States. At that time The Radiant Peace Education Awards only included essays from students in the United States. Now, students submit essays, art, and digital media as well as projects of many kinds. In addition, schools from many different countries have discovered the program online. It is so exciting when boxes and envelopes of Radiant Peace entries arrive from around the world!

In this book you will be reading a selection of award-winning essays and quotes from the first twenty-two years of The Radiant Peace Education Awards program. I am continually inspired by the wisdom and humor of young people. The opportunity to be a part of this program for so many years has been an extraordinary gift in my life. I am honored to be sharing this book with you!

- Ann Healy, Compiler
Executive Director
The Radiant Peace Foundation International, Inc.
August 2013

What is Radiant Peace®?

Radiant Peace® is within us all and is available to everyone. Radiant Peace is natural, whole, harmless, not dualistic, benevolent energy within all our hearts relating us all and making us whole. Radiant Peace transcends the limits of race, age, gender, politics and religion.

From the Purposes of The Radiant Peace Foundation International, Inc. An educational nonprofit founded in 1986

Radiant Peace is the peace that starts with each one of us and can be shared in our daily lives, in our communities and around the world. We all have the capacity to recognize and express the Radiant Peace within each of our hearts. As 6-year-old Claire says, "I carry Radiant Peace around inside of me but sometimes I have to reach down and take it out. Then I can go somewhere and share it."

With this book you will be learning about Radiant Peace from children. Each year, The Radiant Peace Foundation International, Inc. invites students in grades 1-12 to enter The Radiant Peace Education Awards®. Students submit essays, art and special projects based on a Radiant Peace theme such as "Radiant Peace in my World" or "My Commitment to Radiant Peace." Since 1990, this program has reached hundreds of thousands of students across the United States, and, in recent years, in other countries. The essays and quotes in this book are from the first twenty-two years of this program.

Radiant Peace is inherently available to us in all life circumstances. Children tell us Radiant Peace is something greatly needed in our world. They tell us sharing Radiant Peace is something we can all do. And, if you need a few ideas to get you started, here they are...*Radiant Peace®: Wisdom & Tips from Children!*

*The quotes in this book come from students ages 5 to 18.
In order to preserve the originality of each selection,
grammar and spelling are as originally written.*

1 Radiant Peace Is...

Radiant Peace is the love and the happiness that comes from our hearts, and shines over the world.

~ Zachary Maas, age 6, grade 1
Brooker Creek Elementary School, Tarpon Springs, Florida (2010)

Radiant Peace is love. Love is what is in everyone. It's one of the only things that can travel through matter. Love can be connected miles away. Radiant Peace is what helps us live.

~ Riley Gruenthal, age 11, grade 6
Nuestro School, Live Oak, California (2009)

Radiant Peace is all around your life at the beginning, at the middle and at the end of your life. The purpose of Radiant Peace is keeping it in your mind and in your heart all the time.

~ Mario DeArmas, age 9, grade 4
Palm Springs Elementary School, Hialeah, Florida (1992)

Radiant Peace is love so pure and strong that it has the ability to change a life, change a nation, even change the world. It is a smiling face and the sound of laughter. It is ever so simple but endlessly powerful.

~ Olivia Valdes, age 14 , grade 8
Unity School, Delray Beach, Florida (2007)

Radiant Peace is caring about others. I like it. I carry Radiant Peace around inside of me but sometimes I have to reach down and take it out. Then I can go somewhere and share it.

~ Claire Kovarik, age 6, grade 1
Roosevelt Elementary School, Cocoa Beach, Florida (1995)

I think that Radiant Peace is something that we all have inside. We just need to dig it out and then try to help other people. Once you can get Radiant Peace, you need to embrace it.

~ Jessie Nagra, age 11, grade 6
Nuestro School, Live Oak, California (2009)

Radiant Peace is one powerful force. It is combined of love, freedom, generosity, and friendship. Radiant Peace doesn't mean people can't have disagreements. Those are only normal. Children should not be afraid to be outside to play. They should not have to be afraid of war. That is their right of life. To love forever is what Radiant Peace means to me.

~ Karly Nelson, age 9, grade 5
Franklin Elementary School, Pullman, Washington (1992)

Radiant Peace means happiness to share your feelings with one another. Radiant Peace means having joy within yourself. It just makes you shout out! Radiant Peace means victory - to have joy in your heart! Radiant Peace means a warm smile in your heart and on your face! Radiant Peace means making good friends with everyone.

~ Kentia Bradshaw, age 10, grade 6
Martin Luther King Elementary School, Washington, D.C. (1991)

Radiant Peace is the harmony that exists within our hearts.

~ Marisa Ruland, age 12, grade 6
Carwise Middle School, Palm Harbor, Florida (2008)

...The powerful energy of Radiant Peace exceeds any other power that exists, whether it is spiritual, political or monetary. This is because it has no boundaries or restraints to discriminate who can possess it. Once you find the Radiant Peace within yourself, share it with the world....

~ Chandler Thomas, age 16, grade 11
Caroline High School, Milford, Virginia (2010)

Radiant Peace is like love, you can't buy it. Radiant Peace has to come from inside of you, it has to come from the heart. Once you've found it, go spread it with everyone!

~ Lindsey Garven, age 11, grade 6
Chuluota, Florida (1996)

Radiant Peace is loving and laughing. When you love, you spread out energy to others to help them love. When you laugh, you send out energy to make happiness.

~ Courtney Kantor, age 14, grade 8
Unity School, Delray Beach, Florida (2007)

Radiant Peace means harmony to me, people working together, and being able to disagree without fighting with each other. Radiant Peace means a lot of different things, but most of all, Radiant Peace means caring about each other!

~ Andrea Ward, age 8, grade 2
Riley Elementary School, Tallahassee, Florida (1994)

A warm and caring feeling that touches people's
    hearts
A light from deep within us that shatters hatred in
    the dark
A love that breaks down borders and the
    differences that we see
And a passion that gives that love its life and
    stems from you and me.

It's more than just a word, or a cry of defeat and
    surrender
It's the entity that strengthens us and keeps the
    world together
But how can we all reach this point and allow love
    to be released
It starts within the heart of one. It's Radiant Peace.

~ Kyle Koehler, age 17, grade 11
Countryside High School, Clearwater, Florida (2010)

Radiant Peace is love with no boundaries.
It flows in all of us and warms our hearts.

~ Jake Castle, age 7, grade 2
Brooker Creek Elementary School, Tarpon Springs, Florida (2007)

Radiant Peace is the peace that is within us all,
that can be transmitted and radiated from one
person to another. Just as the sun radiates light,
our own hearts can do so, spreading love
and Radiant Peace.

~ Anas Ali El Sawy, age 15, grade 9
Dar El Tarbiah American School, Cairo, Egypt (2012)

Since 1990 more than 250,000 children have participated
in The Radiant Peace Education Awards®

Radiant Peace is not what shows on the outside, but what
shines on the inside. It's how big your heart is and what it
contains. Radiant Peace is one of the main reasons we were
put on this earth.

~ Lindsey Robison, age 12, grade 6
St. Paul Catholic School, St. Petersburg, Florida (2010)

**Radiant Peace is laughter, love and joy that everyone finds
in their heart. There is some in your heart too!**

~ Nevaeh Wright, age 8, grade 3
Azalea Elementary School, St. Petersburg, Florida (2012)

Radiant Peace is the essence that connects us all. From
brother to sister, cousin to cousin, and stranger to
stranger. Radiant Peace is goodwill towards everyone, no
matter their nationality, color or religion. Our hearts are
the same all over the world.

~ Forest McCrosky, age 11, grade 6
Wellington School, St. Petersburg, Florida (2006)

19

Radiant Peace is caring and sharing. Whenever I'm angry I sing a little song so Radiant Peace will come again. Radiant Peace can always be around me. Radiant Peace is wherever you go. Radiant Peace is love.

~ Karin Dynes, age 8, grade 2
Austin Elementary School, Richmond, Texas (1994)

Radiant Peace is losing yourself in a good book and then pretending that you are one of the characters. It is a warm bath that engulfs you and then sets you free. It is a mocha that quenches the thirst.

~ Sarah Michaelsen, age 11, grade 5
John F. Turner Elementary School, Palm Bay, Florida (1999)

Radiant Peace is like love and a big warm hug to me. Radiant Peace is a beautiful shining star.

~ Sydney Leigh Kelley, age 7, grade 2
Wilton Manors Elementary School, Wilton Manors, Florida

Radiant Peace
is what's achieved
when kindness is given;
something only you
can achieve.

~ Connor Bergman, age 11, grade 6
Crest Hill Elementary School, Casper, Wyoming (2008)

Radiant Peace is not disposable; it is eternal.
Unlike normal peace, it cannot be broken.
It is not in just one person; it is in everyone.

~ Dustin Miller, age 9, grade 4
Linwood Elementary School, Oklahoma City, Oklahoma (2006)

To some people Radiant Peace means only an end to wars but to me it means much more than that. Radiant Peace builds up in you and then spreads out. It starts in the heart. Your heart makes it by hearing many kind words and things that make you comfortable and confident in yourself.

~ Vicky Liu, age 9, grade 5
Turtleback Elementary School, San Diego, California (1992)

Radiant Peace is the light that shines from one person to another. It is living, loving and giving. Radiant Peace is in all of us, but not all of us know it...

~ Nada Ahmed Kholeif, age 14, grade 9
Dar El Tarbiah American School, Cairo, Egypt (2012)

Radiant Peace means to care and be kind to others and to love them no matter if they're not perfect to you.

~ Sydnee Robinson, age 8, grade 4
Pinellas Central Elementary School, Pinellas Park, Florida

21

Radiant Peace is doing something nice for someone and having them spread that shining light of peace to others. Radiant Peace is everyone being happy and getting along no matter what we look like or where we live. I wish we could spread Radiant Peace across the world.

~ Arianna Skiadas, age 6, grade 1
Brooker Creek Elementary School, Tarpon Springs, Florida (2007)

Some that say that Radiant Peace is a state of mind. I say it's a state of being.

~ Jeff Stieler, age 11, grade 6
Merritt Island, Florida (1996)

Radiant Peace is something you feel in your heart, not something you say. It is something we have to do together.

~ Ryan Jochum, age 9, grade 5
Greenview Elementary School, Euclid, Ohio (1992)

Radiant Peace is within us all. This invisible force is natural, calm, relaxing and pure wholeness. Radiant Peace walks within our hearts because it is happy and there is a lot of space in there. It radiates in waves all around us within our minds and makes you feel good.

~ John Paul Sieh, age 9, grade 4
Ridgecrest Elementary School, Largo, Florida (2012)

Radiant Peace is giving smiles.

~ Abigail Adkins, age 7, grade 1
Town and Country Elementary, Tampa, Florida (2008)

Radiant Peace is what illuminates inside a person who decides to make a difference.

~ Chris Ruland, age 12, grade 7
Carwise Middle School, Palm Harbor, Florida (2007)

Radiant Peace is like a candle that gives us light and warmth. It has to be struck like a match to work. I try my hardest to light that candle in other people's hearts. I go about striking that match by listening to other people's ideas, by sharing what I think, by understanding why others are the way they are, and not being prejudiced and mean to others with different ethnic backgrounds than me. What makes me feel good is that I know I tried. If everybody tries, it will make me feel even better. If no one tries, the candle will never burn. One candle joined with many others will give light and warmth to our world.

~ Caroline R. Pace, age 11, grade 6
Our Lady of Hope/St. Luke School, Baltimore, Maryland (1996)

Radiant Peace means peace and happiness within that shines on the outside and makes people happy!

~ Dalton Hoch, age 7, grade 1
Wellington School, St. Petersburg, Florida (2009)

Radiant Peace begins with one person and radiates through the world. It sends positive thoughts and love to everyone.

~ Shea Gould, grade 8
Unity School, Delray Beach, Florida (2007)

Radiant Peace to me means showing joy, happiness and having gracefulness by doing what you are supposed to do and being all you can be. Anyone can make a difference.

~ *Pa'shay Leak, age 9, grade 4*
Harbordale YMCA, St. Petersburg, Florida (2012)

Radiant Peace is like a light that comes out of our hearts and spreads into all people's lives.

~ *Andrea Albertson, age 13, grade 7*
PACE - Brantley Hall School, Longwood, Florida (2007)

Radiant Peace is like the sun. We need it to survive.

~ *Melanie DelaConcepcion, age 9*
The Learning Center, Tampa, Florida (2009)

2 Discovering Radiant Peace

Radiant Peace is in everyone and everything. Any person of any religion or race can have Radiant Peace. No matter where you come from or what you believe, we all have the power to shine brightly and spread joy. Radiant Peace comes from your heart. Everyone does have Radiant Peace, but it's the people who are able to see it in everyone who can really change someone's life forever.... To have Radiant Peace is to be able to share your goodness in everything you do.

~ Julianne Franca, age 11, grade 6
St. Timothy Parish School, Miami, Florida (2011)

Radiant Peace is within everyone . . . you just need to look deep inside you. Radiant Peace is a gift you give yourself from your heart.

~ Jenna Meath, age 8, grade 3
Brooker Creek Elementary School, Tarpon Springs, Florida (2009)

No matter who you are, where you are, or what time of the day it is, you can feel Radiant Peace. Because no matter what, Radiant Peace belongs to everyone in his or her hearts waiting for the moment when it will be able to shine through.

~ Lauren Sisak, age 13, grade 7
St. Timothy Parish School, Miami, Florida (2005)

I feel Radiant Peace when my heart feels joyful
and my brain feels love.

~ Amy Jugenheimer, age 9, grade 4
Jacksonville, Florida (1998)

Radiant Peace is something that comes from the heart.
I make Radiant Peace when I walk away from a fight or
help someone who doesn't really like me. If we can all
accept what color people are and the differences then
we can have a good place to live. To make Radiant
Peace with others, you first have to find it in yourself.

~ Harji Rai, age 11, grade 6
Nuestro School, Live Oak, California (2002)

All quotes are from award-winning entries to The Radiant
Peace Education Awards®, open to students worldwide
from schools, home schools and youth groups

Radiant Peace starts with yourself, within your own heart.

~ Lauren Serman, age 11, grade 6
Darnell Coolsman School, Jacksonville, Florida (1998)

Radiant Peace is within each of us. Even if you are
the meanest person, you still have a bit of Radiant
Peace inside of you. But not everyone chooses to
use it....

~ Twan Van Der Togt, grade 5
Anglo-American School of St. Petersburg, Russia (2008)

26

I find Radiant Peace in myself when I wake up each morning and start a brand new day. It brings me Radiant Peace to know that what happened before is in the past. I know that I will start off the day nice and fresh and my brain is ready for a new day of learning.

~ *Julie Spiker, age 10, grade 4*
Brooker Elementary School, Brandon, Florida (1999)

Radiant Peace is not just one big thing, but the many little things we do, see and experience. It is not a complicated thing like so many things in this world; it can be as simple as those carefree moments you spend with your friends. It can be those few moments where you just get to close your eyes and think. Doing what you love and sharing it with others, because Radiant Peace is not just for one person, but for one person to discover and share. That genuine smile you get from a stranger. The random act of kindness you see on the street. One child helping another child work out a problem. Two people in love walking in the park, stopping to tell someone you care about that you love them. All these things are different, but all these things brings us and connect us together. Radiant Peace can come from within, but be experienced by many. Radiant Peace is like a candle; one small flame can disperse the darkness, spreading warmth and light to all around. Radiant Peace is like the calm in the midst of a storm, confidence in the midst of chaos, hope in the midst of adversity. Radiant Peace is the sense of well-being that comes with a mother's kiss, a father's embrace. Radiant Peace is the hope and joy that unites our hearts when we witness the innocent, unselfish act of love or beauty in a child or in nature in the midst of war or tragedy. Radiant Peace is that brief moment when all seems good and right in the world. If you have discovered it, share it.

~ *Zoë Hendricks, age 16, grade 10*
Gibbs High School, St. Petersburg, Florida (2012)

Finding Radiant Peace in myself is like the wind trying to open a space. Sometimes it is hard and sometimes it is easy. Radiant Peace is like joy that flows around your heart or a diamond that sparkles beautifully with all of the rainbow colors.

~ Rayna Saint-Jean, age 10, grade 5
Linda Lentin Elementary School, North Miami, Florida (1999)

In order to have Radiant Peace in our lives, we have to look within everybody's heart, starting with our own. We have to see beyond people to see the light that shines through their soul.

~ Lizzie Milner, age 13, grade 8
Nuestro School, Live Oak, California (2011)

... Radiant Peace is the chain reaction that happens when you say positive motivating words to everyone you pass...

~ Jared Geller, age 11, grade 6
Unity School, Delray Beach, Florida (2012)

To find Radiant Peace, first, I look inside myself to find what I like to do. When I find it, I go and do it. Lots of times I go out and look at the clouds. The pure white clouds purify me from anger. So, in other words, I find what I like and I do it. Follow these steps. It might work for you. Go ahead. Try it. Find Radiant Peace inside of you.

~ Benjamin, age 10, grade 5
Challenger 7 Elementary School, Cocoa, Florida (1998)

Radiant Peace begins with what is in your heart and soul. Radiant Peace helps you show your real identity and helps you accomplish anything. Radiant Peace is love and caring that we can share around the world with others.

~ Jasmine Sims, age 11, grade 6
Harbordale YMCA, St. Petersburg, Florida (2012)

You can find Radiant Peace only if you let your heart shine and believe in yourself!

~ Estill Loyd, age 10, grade 4
Lakeview Fundamental Elementary School, St. Petersburg, Florida (2009)

There are several ways I find Radiant Peace within me. I can talk with my family and close friends. I can go into my room and think and pray. People can tell you about Radiant Peace, but you have to find it in your own heart... When I find this Radiant Peace in myself, I'm never afraid.

~ LeeAnn Nawrocki, age 12, grade 6
St. Mark's Academy, Cocoa, Florida (1999)

Radiant Peace means friendship and love, caring and understanding. Radiant Peace is in every quick little kiss, and every great big hug. You might find it in a misty rainbow, or in a beautiful sunset. But you will always find it in your heart. It may be right on top of everything, or way, way down at the bottom... Radiant Peace may be just around the corner, or ages and ages to go. But it will come. Radiant Peace will come.

~ Michal Telem, age 11, grade 5
Krieger Schechter Middle School, Baltimore, Maryland (1993)

For me, Radiant Peace isn't just having no wars, it's showing love and respect to the people around you. You can't hold Radiant Peace or touch it, but you can show it.

~ Alexis Weiss, age 10
Wellington School, St. Petersburg, Florida (2004)

If you are in a bad mood, dig deep in your soul for a happy thought as a farmer digs holes in the soil. You will see it makes you feel Radiant Peace. Being a Radiant Peacemaker is the best thing you can be!

~ Andrea Alhadari, age 12, grade 6
St. Timothy Parish School, Miami, Florida (2001)

I find Radiant Peace within me by deeply looking in my heart.

~ Casey, age 8, grade 3
Highland Oaks Elementary School, Miami, Florida (1998)

Radiant Peace is the beauty that someone has inside of them. Radiant Peace can be shown in many ways. It can be shown by caring for someone. It can also be shown by listening to someone when they need someone to talk to or just by lending a helping hand. Everyone has Radiant Peace within them and it can make someone extraordinary. Radiant Peace can be found all over the world.

~ Sebastian Fernandez, age 11, grade 6
St. Timothy Parish School, Miami, Florida (2011)

Something that really helps me find Radiant Peace is helping others. The feeling I get is pure energy. When I help others I feel extremely useful.

~ Lindsey Young, age 10, grade 4
Ojus Elementary School, North Miami Beach, Florida (1999)

As we get to know ourselves more and the people around us longer, we notice that we have many things in common. We all cry, laugh, hurt, fall, rise up. That's common throughout the whole globe, no matter what background we have, we're all equal in one way or another. One of the most common things that brings everybody closer together is Radiant Peace. Radiant Peace is big like the sky, where the sun is always shining, maybe in different seasons, but it still has its own glow. In order to have Radiant Peace in our lives, we have to look within everybody's heart, starting with our own. We have to see beyond people to see the light that shines through their soul....

~ Romina Buna, age 17, grade 11
Countryside High School, Clearwater, Florida (2010)

Radiant Peace is somewhere in our hearts, even if you don't know it. It's in you, it's in me, it's in everyone!

~ Marissa Guedes, age 12, grade 7
St. Timothy Parish School, Miami, Florida (2009)

I can find Radiant Peace in myself by looking into my heart and finding my compassionate side. I can show Radiant Peace by caring for and helping people.

~ Alaina, age 10, grade 5
Quail Summit Elementary School, Diamond Bar, California (1998)

Radiant Peace is children having fun, a mother holding her baby for the first time, a dad teaching his son how to catch. It is a gentle smile given to someone who is having a rough day. Radiant Peace is spread through laughter, smiles or just a simple hello. We live in a beautiful world full of Radiant Peace. All we have to do is notice it.

~ Sara Malinka, age 18, grade 12
Countryside High School, Clearwater, Florida (2010)

Radiant Peace starts inside of ourselves and is spread through kindness. If everyone could find a way to show someone else kindness everyday, then Radiant Peace could radiate throughout the whole world.

~ James Allen, age 10, grade 4
Ridgecrest Elementary School, Largo, Florida (2007)

Radiant Peace is love and kindness and helping others, like putting a band-aid on a little kid that's hurt.

~ Sarah Briskey, age 9, grade 3
Graebner Elementary School, Sterling Heights, Michigan (2007)

Radiant Peace is like getting set free from a motocross start gate. It is released from everyone's heart and soul, just like the bike from the start gate.

~ Alex Fisk, age 13, grade 8
PACE - Brantley Hall School, Longwood, Florida (2007)

Being twelve years old isn't easy, but finding Radiant Peace within myself can be - I just have to remember where to look.

~ Hunter, age 12, grade 6
Seaside Neighborhood School, Seaside, Florida (1998)

Radiant Peace is a warmth, spreading in your body when people are kind towards you, or when you know you've done something good yourself. It's a feeling everybody has and gives. But don't get me wrong, it's not only a feeling. It's an action, as well - the action of respecting and caring.

Getting Radiant Peace is wonderful. It makes you feel appreciated and worth something. One of my best experiences of getting Radiant Peace is when I first started in the school I go to now. I almost didn't know any English, and I was, well, not really shy, but very quiet. I spoke very rarely. But even though I wasn't talking very much to my classmates, they always called "Hi!" to me when I came to school, and made me feel welcome and happy.

But something that might feel even better is giving Radiant Peace. It feels great seeing people becoming happy when you appreciate them. I hope I'm giving Radiant Peace to people around me, because I get so much from so many.

~ Clara Scholander, age 12, grade 7
Anglo-American School of St. Petersburg, Russia (2008)

When I need to find Radiant Peace, I go into a quiet place and rest. In that place, I gather my thoughts and think about something different than the problem that I may be having. I make up a place in my mind and I put Radiant Peace thoughts there... I think that if all is well and everyone can find their Radiant Peace, then the world will be a better place for both me and you.

~ Kendra Nicole Key, age 10, grade 5
Woodland Forrest Elementary School, Tuscaloosa, Alabama (1998)

Radiant Peace is here and there.
Radiant Peace is everywhere.
Open your hearts and you will see,
There are no limits to where it will be.

~ Jenny Embree, age 11, grade 6
St. Paul Catholic School, St. Petersburg, Florida (2011)

Radiant Peace means being joyful and happy for what you have and who you are. Radiant Peace is loving your personality and life.

~ Cynthia Vankleeck, age 9, grade 4
Perkins Elementary School, St. Petersburg, Florida (2008)

Radiant Peace to me is when you smile at someone and they smile back.

~ Quinton Hines, age 7, grade 2
Bay Point Elementary School, St. Petersburg, Florida (2012)

Radiant Peace is like a radiator spreading its heat waves of love and friendship all over the world. Radiant Peace is like the line in our smiles that curls.

~ Catelynn Wood, age 10, grade 5
Linwood Elementary School, Oklahoma City, Oklahoma (2007)

Radiant Peace is not in one but all.
You just have to look for it!

~ Anthony Lynch, age 9, grade 4
Lakeview Fundamental Elementary School, St. Petersburg, Florida (2008)

3 Commitment to Radiant Peace

Radiant Peace comes from within our hearts. It comes from love and kindness. If we show love to all people, animals and plants, it will spread around the earth like a wildfire! If one person shows love to two people and they show love to two people, it will continue on and on and that is Radiant Peace.

~ Ella Wiebe, age 8, grade 3
Castaic Elementary School, Castaic, California (2012)

Radiant Peace in this world is very important. Radiant Peace is the thing that holds the world together from chaos. I express my Radiant Peace by not harming anyone physically and emotionally.

~ Yong Naccaratto, age 13, grade 7
Miami Community Charter School, Florida City, Florida (2008)

It takes each one of us to create Radiant Peace in our own little world, wherever our world is. Radiant Peace is a big circle and everyone is a part of it. We have our whole lives to make it bigger.

~ Lacey Scoot, age 8, grade 3
Bayshore Elementary School, Bradenton, Florida (1996)

Smiling and laughter are great ways to spread Radiant Peace, and I know I can help it catch on all over the world, one person at a time.

~ Kevin N. Vu, age 12, grade 6
James Weldon Johnson Middle School, Jacksonville, Florida (2000)

Sometimes finding Radiant Peace is a challenge, but I try never to give up! It takes only one person to start Radiant Peace. When I have made a difference, I can feel the happiness inside myself. You never know what you can do until you try.

~ Emily Elizabeth Caro, age 10, grade 5
Levi Fry Intermediate School, Texas City, Texas (1998)

Radiant Peace spreads, if one person has peace with themself, then it will rub off on people around them. Radiant Peace starts with one person. Radiant Peace starts with me.

~ Angela Hardy, age 10, grade 5
McKamy Elementary School, Carrollton, Texas (1996)

Your soul is a major part in Radiant Peace, for way down somewhere there is a great serenity and kindness. If we listen to it and follow it there would be harmony in the world, and we would all be friends and neighbors. The next time you are in a fight, find this Radiant Peace and follow it and see where it leads you.

~ Lael Harrison, age 10, grade 5
Harborview Elementary School, Juneau, Alaska (1991)

I am a Radiant Peacemaker when I help a friend. If someone is lonely, I can play with them to make them happy. If someone trips, I can help them up. If someone is hurt or bruised, I can get help. If someone cries, I can give them a hug.

~ Evan Christopher, age 8, grade 3
Mt. Vernon Elementary School, St. Petersburg, Florida (2010)

One positive way of being a Radiant Peacemaker is to help others in their time of despair. Be a friend to someone who has no friends. I am a Radiant Peacemaker when I care.

~ Ariane Christina Swick, age 13, grade 8
St. Paul Catholic School, St. Petersburg, Florida (2000)

To understand the true meaning of Radiant Peace, what you do is much more important than what you say. We can tell each other that Radiant Peace is very important, but not until we actually practice it will it really begin to make a difference. We are not born mean and violent people. This way of living is something that we are taught. Making Radiant Peace in our world is not easy. Everyone will have to work together to change the way things already are.

~ Sarah Eriksson, grade 8, age 13
Terrace Community School, Tampa, Florida (2002)

Radiant Peace is giving a 28 dollar bill to everyone even if I do not know them at all.

~ Tess Polites, age 6, grade 1
Brooker Creek Elementary School, Tarpon Springs, Florida (2012)

What does Radiant Peace mean to me? Radiant Peace means that you have inner peace, the peace within yourself. It also means that you are happy with yourself and how you are because before you can have Radiant Peace with others you have to build Radiant Peace within yourself.

~ Terrell Dukes, age 15, grade 9
Gibbs High School, St. Petersburg, Florida (2007)

Radiant Peace is letting people know you got their backs, even if they never got yours.

~ *Reina Maria Rivera, age 9, grade 3*
Town and Country Elementary School, Tampa, Florida (2008)

Finding Radiant Peace within myself is something I find I have to work on every day. For me, it's not as hard to find the Radiant Peace as it is to keep it. Somehow, knowing that I've tried being the best person I can be, makes other parts of life easier. Radiant Peace, to me, means that I'm happy with myself and what I've become.

~ *Allison, age 12, grade 6*
Melbourne, Florida (1998)

———————————— ❋ ————————————

One mile of the Tahoe Rim Trail in Nevada is
dedicated to Radiant Peace®

———————————— ❋ ————————————

What is Radiant Peace? Some think it's what you give off when you do something nice. Others think it's what people give to others as they help them, or share something, or simply smile. I think it's the fuel that runs your life. You can use this fuel two ways. One - you can keep it inside all day, or, two - you can share it with people everywhere. If you choose choice one, nobody gets to know you, and you don't make any friends. If you choose choice two, you make lots of friends, and lots of people like you. I always advise people to share as much Radiant Peace as they can....

~ *Jonas Olson, age 11, grade 5*
Ridgecrest Elementary School, Largo, Florida (2010)

I feel Radiant Peace in my heart when I know that I have helped someone do something they think they can't do. It is like making something impossible possible. I know that others are being helped. And that is what makes me have Radiant Peace in my heart.

~ *Andy Davis, age 8, grade 2*
Holy Family School, St. Petersburg, Florida (1997)

I have lots of times when I need to find Radiant Peace in myself. There are some troubles I just can't handle with anger. When I do have anger I look and search until I find Radiant Peace. And when I do find it, I spend some time with it. Radiant Peace doesn't always come easily. Sometimes it's deep down inside me suffocating from anger or something else it's buried in. When I find my Radiant Peace I feel happier and lighter.

~ *Laura Moore, age 10, grade 5*
Cape View Elementary School, Cape Canaveral, Florida (1999)

I believe that everyone is born with Radiant Peace.... I am a Radiant Peacemaker by being a good, caring, understanding, non-judgmental and compassionate friend to all. I know that this is very hard to do, but I certainly try my best. I do this by being there when someone needs a helping hand or just someone to listen to them.

~ *Carolina Thompson, age 9, grade 3*
Castaic Elementary School, Castaic, California (2011)

Radiant Peace is being kind and loving. Radiant Peace is being a helpful friend. If I laugh at other people and call them names, I am not showing my Radiant Peace. When I help people the best I can that would be showing my Radiant Peace. To stand up for what I believe in is right, even when others make fun of me is how I find Radiant Peace within myself.

~ Andrew Bernier, age 10, grade 4
St. Patrick School, Tampa, Florida (1998)

I am a Radiant Peacemaker. When I was at the park with my friend, she felt left out because nobody was playing with her. So I went right over and asked her to play a game. So we went to the slides and made our own secret hideout and then played on the swings.

~ Kendall Crider, age 6, grade 1
Brooker Creek Elementary School, Tarpon Springs, Florida (2009)

Radiant Peace cannot be bought, for it is entirely free. Radiant Peace is pure from the heart, peace made by you and me.

~ Madeleine M. Jarvis, age 9, grade 4
Leila G. Davis Elementary School, Clearwater, Florida (2008)

I help the world have Radiant Peace by caring about others and my family. Each of us has work to do. Each of us has something to give. Caring about someone when they are down is something I can do, even though I'm only 9. I think Radiant Peace is in everyone's heart, but some people just don't let it out.

~ Sabrina Kidd, age 10, grade 4
Cocoa, Florida (1995)

Since the September 11 terrorist attack, the world has needed an extra boost of Radiant Peace and happiness. My contribution will be to be friendly to other people that I meet. Even if I am the only one to participate in my theory, it will affect many other people.

This is my theory: if one person is kind to one different person every day for a year, that equals 365 people. Over a time span of ten years, that equals 36,500 people! If one million people try this, it will equal 3,650,000,000 people! To advertise my theory, I will tell my friends about it. Then I will ask them to tell other people. After that, the pattern will simply continue. With all these people being kind, there might not be any more terrorists. So in conclusion, please try my theory and be kind.

~ Tiffany Heaton, age 11, grade 6
Walker Elementary School, Northport, Alabama (2002)

I wish I could fly
through the clear sky
carrying Radiant Peace and joy
in a serene heart
to those who do not have it.

~ Ambra Spinsante, age 13
Numana, Italy (1997)

To find the Radiant Peace in me, I must look, I must see. To find the Radiant Peace in the world, we need to love and care.

~ Veronica Clanzy, age 9, grade 4
Ridgecrest Elementary School, Largo, Florida (2009)

Radiant Peace is like a circle. Each person is part of the circle. We have our whole lives to make the circle bigger. Each of us has work to do. Each of us has special gifts like being understanding, being helpful, fixing things, being calm, cheerful, happy, and thankful. Each person is needed. If one is missing, the circle is broken. Together we work for Radiant Peace.

~ Jennifer Reynolds, age 8, grade 3
The Benjamin School, North Palm Beach, Florida (1995)

Nothing in the world is better than Radiant Peace. Radiant Peace is the biggest thing worth living for. Radiant Peace is the best thing in life.

~ Kara Cox, age 10, grade 4
Mt. Vernon Enola Elementary School, Enola, Arkansas (1991)

I make Radiant Peace in my heart when I care for people. I like all kinds of people and I am kind to everybody. When I know people think good thoughts about me it makes me feel good. Thinking good thoughts about others makes me feel Radiant Peace in my heart.

~ Shamari Griffin, grade 2, age 7
Vance Elementary School, Vance, Alabama (1997)

I find Radiant Peace in myself by helping someone who's in need because I know that there is one less person in the world who's in pain.

~ Amanda Charles, age 10, grade 5
Holy Family Catholic School, St. Petersburg, Florida (1999)

I think I am a Radiant Peacemaker when I help others. I know how it feels to help someone because everyday I tutor a little girl in the first grade. She has a hard time reading. Sometimes I get irritated when she can't figure out a simple word like "boy". But when I tutor her I remember that I'm helping her accomplish something that will make her feel better about herself. When she gets older I hope she will pass her gift of reading on to someone else that needs her help. I know I did not stop a war or anything like that, but I still feel like I'm a Radiant Peacemaker in my own way.

~ *Ulescia Prince, age 12, grade 6*
Vance Elementary School, Vance, Alabama (2001)

Radiant Peace is shining the happyness on everybody. I want to be a good leader of Radiant Peace.

~ *Lynaida Rodriguez, age 10, grade 4*
Town and Country Elementary School, Tampa, Florida (2007)

I think that Radiant Peace is like an echo. If you send it out it will be repeated over and over again. I try to treat people fairly, and make them feel important. I try to treat them with kindness. I think that if I start an echo of Radiant Peace, other people will take notice. Maybe they would start an echo of their own. Each echo would grow larger and larger and spread across the world. One small act of kindness can go along way. One person can start an echo of Radiant Peace and watch it grow....and grow.... and grow.

~ *Dominic Bruno, age 10, grade 5*
Hopatcong, New Jersey (1995)

If each person cared about each other like brothers and sisters, and if no one would fight, this will be a better planet for you and me to live on.

~ Elena Gordillo, age 11, grade 6
M. A. Milam Elementary School, Hialeah, Florida (1996)

Whenever I'm peaceful, I can really tell I'm alive inside. Sometimes, it's hard to find Radiant Peace in myself, but when I do, I can really tell. My spirit comes alive like sparks from fireworks.

~ Maureen, age 12, grade 6
St. Timothy Parish School, Miami, Florida (1999)

4 Radiant Peace in Daily Life

Radiant Peace is all about what you do. Loving your neighbors spreads Radiant Peace. Hugging your competitors spreads Radiant Peace. Kissing your granpa spreads Radiant Peace....

~ Joseph Zhong, age 8, grade 2
Swanson Elementary School, Omaha, Nebraska (2011)

I help make Radiant Peace by trying to be kind to others. I try to be kind to everyone. If we are all kind to each other we can all help.

~ Hali Paul, age 6, grade 1
Vance Elementary School, Vance, Alabama (2002)

Happy, bright, colorful and loving are all words to describe Radiant Peace. It is showing kindness to everyone and everything in the world. Smiling at a stranger or doing a good deed are ways to spread Radiant Peace around to everyone... Just like how a rainbow can cheer us up so can a simple smile. By spreading Radiant Peace through a smile more than one person can be effected by a chain reaction of smiles. Give a smile, get a smile. Together we can show Radiant Peace.

~ Katherine McGrory, age 9, grade 3
Castaic Elementary School, Castaic, California (2012)

Radiant Peace starts when you wake up every morning with a smile on your face, go out into the world and see the good in everyone.

~ Dominika Dzurny, age 12, grade 6
St. Paul Catholic School, St. Petersburg, Florida (2012)

To achieve Radiant Peace people must be honest, trust each other, and be happy with who they are. For people to be happy with who they are they must focus on positive things.

~ Johnny George, age 12, grade 6
Unity School, Delray Beach, Florida (1996)

...To me, Radiant Peace is the person who smiles at you after you had a bad day, the person who picks up your books when you dropped them, the person that shows they care about you by asking about your day, the car that stops when you're trying to cross the street, the person that picks up the trash on the ground, the stranger that returns your lost wallet, the child that gives his favorite toy to his younger brother, the guy at the gas station that gives the young seventeen-year-old money so he can drive home, the person that stops to feed the hungry, the firefighter that risks her life so she can save a child, the dog that greets you when you walk into your home, the teacher that stops so that she can make sure you understand what you are learning, the person on your team that gives you a hand when you're on the ground, the coach that gives up many hours of his week to his team, the neighbor that lets you have the ingredient that you are missing in a recipe, the vet that cures your beloved pet, and the doctor that saves your friend's life.

To me, Radiant Peace is the kind actions that we do for one another. Radiant Peace is us looking out for each other. Radiant Peace is us.

~ Erin Waterman, age 14, grade 8
St. Paul Catholic School, St. Petersburg, Florida (2008)

You can do anything if your heart is in it. To me Radiant Peace is like a team of people. When someone doesn't care and doesn't do their part the team is ruined. Radiant Peace can be taking time to talk to a neighbor or caring for a sick friend or even telling your mom or dad you love them. I can help the world achieve Radiant Peace by giving all I have, and putting love and compassion in it.

~ Kristin Prichard, age 10, grade 5
Richmond, Texas (1995)

I think Radiant Peace is forgiving each other.

~ Thomas Ranalli, age 7, grade 2
Azalea Elementary School, St. Petersburg, Florida (2012)

I express Radiant Peace simply by smiling. Smiling makes people feel welcomed. It's like saying, "Here I am, be my friend."

~ Jose Perez, age 13, grade 7
Miami Community Charter School, Florida City, Florida (2008)

I find Radiant Peace in myself by laughing. I love laughing. It gives me a tingly feeling and I heard that if you laugh 100 times it is worth 10 minutes of aerobic exercise. I also enjoy making other people laugh. It has to be the funnest thing in the world.

~ Cody Malm, age 11, grade 5
Levi Fry Intermediate School, Texas City, Texas (1999)

I can help the world have more Radiant Peace by smiling. Have you ever been walking in your neighborhood, and you were down, and then, all of a sudden someone passes by and smiles at you. Doesn't that make you all warm inside? I know it really makes my day when someone takes the time for that little gesture: a smile. Everyone should smile more. Our world has lost some of the sense of unity it should have. Smiling can make a world of difference. If for example, you fall and start crying, you feel better when someone smiles at you and says it's okay. When you give up and you feel like you just can't, if someone smiles at you, the courage to try surges through your body and you feel that everything is okay. I'd say if people smile a little more, more Radiant Peace would be in our world.

~ Staci Edelstein, age 10, grade 5
Coral Gables Elementary School, Coral Gables, Florida (1996)

Radiant Peace Tips:
1. Be friendly
2. Get as many friends as possible
3. Keep at least one friend

~ Jared Morgan, grade 4
Vance Elementary School, Vance, Alabama (1992)

Radiant Peace is when you make someone laugh. You have this feeling that you put a huge smile on someone's face. This is an awesome feeling!

~ Princess Bowen, age 9, grade 3
Town and Country Elementary School, Tampa, Florida (2007)

50

Close your eyes and think about how you can spread Radiant Peace. One way is by giving someone a sweet compliment. This would make someone else feel good, and chances are they would then give someone else a sweet compliment. Think about all the things you can do to make this world a better place. There are 6.6 billion people out there so let's get working!

~ Christina Tournant, age 9, grade 4
Ridgecrest Elementary School, Largo, Florida (2007)

I find Radiant Peace when I'm listening to soft music because my ears love to settle down.

~ Riesha Bridgewater, age 7, grade 2
Miami, Florida (1999)

Radiant Peace in my life is like a group of bubbles. They shine and glow working together to make a wonderful scene as they drift through the sky like diamonds. People are the same. If you give a person a compliment, their glimmer will make the world a nicer place.

~ Amelia G. Jobe, age 9, grade 3
Camarillo Academy of Progressive Education, Camarillo, California (2012)

Radiant Peace means liking myself and not trying to be what others want me to be, but being what I want me to be. Being a Radiant Peacemaker is important to me because it can make my life and other people's lives better.

~ Maygan Smitherman, age 11, grade 6
Vance Elementary School, Vance, Alabama (2000)

Radiant Peace is holding people up when they are down.

~ Jack Digney, grade 8
Unity School, Delray Beach, Florida (2007)

I am a Radiant Peacemaker when I show compassion to others whenever they are feeling morose. I try to ask what's wrong and help out however I can. It only takes a few minutes to stop and help someone in need to spread Radiant Peace. Even just having someone take the time to ask what's wrong can save someone's life.

~ Hunter Hale, age 16, grade 11
Miami Community Charter School, Florida City, Florida (2012)

When you worry, you need to quickly drop it. Worry is definitely not the definition of Radiant Peace!

~ Kate, age 9, grade 4
Apollo Elementary School, Titusville, Florida (1999)

I find Radiant Peace within myself when I watch my hamster crawl in his tubes. It makes me forget about everything. Riding my bike helps me find Radiant Peace in myself. When the wind swishes past me I think I am flying without wings and watching over the city. Swimming makes me feel Radiant Peace also. When I go under the water I feel weightless. I think I am drifting in space and looking at the Earth.

~ Bradley Coleman, age 9, grade 3
Renaissance School, Lakeland, Florida (1998)

Radiant Peace can be spread by everyone to make the world a better place to live in. One example of how I spread Radiant Peace is when I help others and do not expect anything back.

~ Aysha Patel, age 6, grade 1
Our Lady of Hope/St. Luke School, Baltimore, Maryland (2008)

The Radiant Peace Foundation International, Inc. is a 501(c)(3) educational nonprofit founded in 1986 with headquarters in St. Petersburg, Florida

Finding Radiant Peace in myself is very healthy for my body and mind. When I find Radiant Peace in myself I can deal with everything and accept things the way they are. Radiant Peace brings positive energy to my life and everything around me.

~ Cristina Enriquez, age 12, grade 7
St. Timothy Parish School, Miami, Florida (2001)

I would like to share with you ways I find Radiant Peace. One way is talking to myself. I talk to myself mostly when I have a tough problem. If the problem is a difference of opinion, talking to the other person usually leads to more fighting. Also when I talk to myself in a quiet place I can concentrate. Sometimes I think I am the best person for me to talk to.

~ Anthony, age 9, grade 4
Apollo Elementary School, Titusville, Florida (1998)

Radiant Peace is inside all of us. Everyone is capable of sharing Radiant Peace, from a small child to adults and into elder years. Radiant Peace can be as simple as opening a door for someone or as big as starting a charity for those in need. When you express Radiant Peace, you can feel it inside; glowing and warm. Radiant Peace is inside of all of us just waiting to release and spread itself.

~ Josh Stevenson, age 8, grade 3
Castaic Elementary School, Castaic, California (2011)

Radiant Peace is as simple as saying, "Hi!" to your bus driver when you get on the bus.

~ Samir Rajani, age 9, grade 4
Ridgecrest Elementary School, Largo, Florida (2009)

I make Radiant Peace in the world when I pray for others, when I am kind to others, and when I help others. I make the world a lot better when I help others up when they are down. The world has more Radiant Peace with me because I will let no one down. The world needs me, and I'm there to help. I put a lot of frowns upside down.

~ Nicholas Dvorak, age 8, grade 3
Our Lady of Hope/St. Luke School, Baltimore, Maryland (2003)

Radiant Peace can happen everywhere. Just make it happen! You can do it. Anyone can. Come on, let's spread Radiant Peace!

~ Kylie Grant, age 7, grade 1
Summit-Questa Montessori School, Davie, Florida (2008)

If anybody can be counted on to make Radiant Peace in the world, it's me! My ideas are simple: stop spreading rumors, accept people for who they are, and make friends with everyone. First, I can accomplish this by not spreading nasty, heartbreaking rumors. When rumors start, it's virtually impossible to stop them. Even a simple rumor can ruin someone's life instantly. Think before you speak. Another vital thing I will do is make FRIENDS!! I will accept people for what they are, not what I want them to be. I'll show loyalty and stand up for friends. I'll introduce them to each other, creating a "Chain of Radiant Peace." My accomplishments aren't stopping wars or anything like that, because it starts with me. Maybe this plan can start a world living in "Radiant Peace and Harmony."

~ Justin Trotter, age 12, grade 6
John F. Turner Elementary School, Palm Bay, Florida (1997)

I find Radiant Peace in myself by being my own person and not acting like anyone but me.

~ Allison, age 12, grade 6
St. Philip's Episcopal School, Coral Gables, Florida (1998)

Baking cookies is one of my favorite things to do, so I decided I could put this talent into helping bring Radiant Peace. Once, when I baked my irresistible chocolate chip peanut butter cookies, and brought them to our neighbors, we started a new friendship. Remember... people loving people brings Radiant Peace.

~ Jenny Hendriksen, age 9, grade 4
Academie Da Vinci, Dunedin, Florida (1999)

Radiant Peace is like a person saying "Hello." Radiant Peace is like waking up to another bright, beautiful, sunny day. Radiant Peace is like making friends on the first day of school. Radiant Peace feels like you are never alone. Radiant Peace is true freedom.... Radiant Peace is the best thing you could ever imagine.

~ Kaitlin McKay-Cohen, age 7, grade 3
Ridgecrest Elementary School, Largo, Florida (2011)

Radiant Peace is when I smile at someone and they smile back. These smiles hug our hearts.

~ Isabella James, age 6, grade 1
Brooker Creek Elementary School, Tarpon Springs, Florida (2009)

I can help the world to achieve Radiant Peace by having fun with my friends and getting along with other people. By doing this, if someone mean and grouchy is with a bunch of people who are having fun and getting along, it is hard for someone to stay mean and grouchy. Then that person would spread their happiness, and the cycle would continue.

~ Sheena Kwaterski, age 12, grade 6
Gibraltar School, Fish Creek, Wisconsin (1996)

Radiant Peace in the world can be better achieved if everyone would learn to love and live with one another. Also, don't be too rushed to enjoy the little things in life. Smiles, hugs and kind words help spread Radiant Peace.

~ Michael G., age 10, grade 5
Baton Rouge, Louisiana (1991)

56

To me spreading Radiant Peace is easy because all you have to do is have a smile on your face at all times and be kind and generous to everyone!

~ Mercedes Martin, age 11, grade 5
Town and Country Elementary School, Tampa, Florida (2007)

Visit The Radiant Peace Place online at

www.radiantpeace.org

How can I help make Radiant Peace in the new millennium? I can make friends with everyone, (or at least try). I can share things with people. I can break up fights. I could go on and on naming things that I could do, but the main thing I could do is not judge people. Don't judge people from their race, clothes, and how they talk. I think everyone has something they dislike about themselves. For example, I don't like wearing glasses, but I have to because I'm blind without them. Judging people hurts their feelings, and makes them think negative thoughts about themselves. Making fun of people is like judging them. What I could do is not to judge anyone, and tell my friends they could tell their friends not to judge people and so on, and that's how I would make a millennium with more Radiant Peace.

~ Jordan Guss, age 10, grade 5
Levi Fry Intermediate School, Texas City, Texas (1999)

How can a little boy in Richmond, Virginia, help world peace? I can be a role model for younger children. Kids are the future of our world. If children see me being nice to others, they'll see that violence isn't right. Love and Radiant Peace are spread from heart to heart, like candles lighting each other. If those candles are blown out, there is not peace but hate. To spread that flame, I can congratulate the other team after a baseball game. I can share with my friends and family. I can do so much for Radiant Peace by just being kind and caring. I want to spread that burning candle in my heart to other people. By being a role model, I can show others how to be kind. And if everybody was kind and caring, there would be Radiant Peace in this world.

~ Danny Melson, age 10, grade 5
Dumbarton Elementary School, Richmond, Virginia (1997)

Sometimes the best reaction is no reaction. Thoughtlessness can lead to hurt feelings, misunderstandings, or war. Being a Radiant Peacemaker is important and it begins with me. Who knows, one day I may change history.

~ Jason Morris, age 13, grade 8
Roulhac Middle School, Chipley, Florida (2000)

I spread Radiant Peace when I help somebody feel better. It's like there is a wall around somebody's heart. But Radiant Peace breaks through the wall and gets into their heart. That makes them have Radiant Peace. And that helps me spread Radiant Peace.

~ Madeline Ford, age 6, grade 1
Ridgecrest Elementary School, Largo, Florida (2007)

One way I spread Radiant Peace is by playing with the new kids so they feel included in the school.

~ Allessandra Sorenson, age 8, grade 3
Graebner Elementary School, Sterling Heights, Michigan (2007)

Everyone experiences Radiant Peace every minute of their lives, but most don't notice it. Radiant Peace cannot be explained with a single definition. It isn't something that can be put in a box, dissected, analyzed and put back together. Radiant Peace just is. When you get caught up in your life complications and emotions, when you take a deep breath and accept things the way they are and recognize a feeling of serenity - that is Radiant Peace. It doesn't mean you don't have to work out your troubles, but it means that there is never the need to worry about it, never the need to get caught up, like a fish struggling in a fisherman's net. Radiant Peace allows us to relax and work things out systematically, and even when there is no solution, Radiant Peace will still be there to support us, allowing us to smile in the face of trouble.

~ Charmaine Chu Wen Lo, age 15, grade 11
James Ruse Agricultural High School, Sydney, Australia (2011)

We shine brightest when we share Radiant Peace.

~ Victoria Rogers, age 8, grade 3
Freddy Gonzalez Elementary School, Edinburg, Texas (2012)

I make Radiant Peace when I see people fighting and ask, "what are you fighting about?" If it was over a ball, then I'll say, "Let's share the ball by kicking it to each other." I also make Radiant Peace when I tell my brain, "Calm down, Robby" when I'm feeling mad.

~ Robert Price, age 6, grade 1
Our Lady of Hope/St. Luke School, Baltimore, Maryland (1999)

Radiant Peace is what I feel in my heart when I hear my cat purring or when I am sitting down with a good book. Radiant Peace is when I am spending time with family or friends or just being creative with myself. It's all part of having Radiant Peace.

~ Annabelle Salmeron, age 9, grade 4
Perkins Elementary School, St. Petersburg, Florida (2008)

Radiant Peace is neither prejudice nor bias. It is not set to any one person or race. Radiant Peace is the natural feeling inside us to do good, the desire that we all have to promote peace that radiates to the chaos around us. Radiant Peace should not be locked up inside us, but should be circulated from one person to another for all to enjoy.

~ Jonathan Carbungco, age 13, grade 8
St. Paul Catholic School, St. Petersburg, Florida (2007)

Radiant Peace is having a great day of my life!

~ Imam Hasan, age 7, grade 2
Temple Terrace Elementary School, Temple Terrace, Florida (2012)

5 Radiant Peace and Family

When you drop a pebble in water the ripples spread out and get bigger and bigger. If we each work to get along in our families, the circle of Radiant Peace will grow bigger. It can spread to our friends, school, community and, eventually, the world.

~ Joshua Hamilton, age 11, grade 5
Port St. John, Florida (1996)

I feel Radiant Peace being with my parents. We have hot cocoa on rainy nights. On those nights I get a blanket from my bed and cuddle with my parents. They make me feel safe inside. I get my dog and cat, and we all snuggle together.

~ Lindsey Massimo, age 7, grade 2
Meadowlane Elementary School, West Melbourne, Florida (1999)

Radiant Peace is what unites us as a human race. It is energy within our hearts that encourages us to put aside our differences in race, age, gender, etc., and think of everyone as our brothers or sisters.

~ Ally Zamitalo, age 12, grade 8
St. Paul Catholic School, St. Petersburg, Florida (2012)

I am a Radiant Peacemaker when I make my mom laugh after she has had a stressful day at work and when my dad needs someone to remind him that he will feel better soon. I am a Radiant Peacemaker when I'm simply ME.

~ Alexandra Pagliery, age 11, grade 6
St. Timothy Parish School, Miami, Florida (2001)

61

I first learned about the feeling of Radiant Peace talking with my grandmother. Whenever she was around I always felt Radiant Peace. The feeling of Radiant Peace I felt with my grandmother was like a warm feeling you get from a hug from your dad at the end of a long day. Listening to other people's ideas, treating people with care, learning from others, and following your heart are all special ways my grandmother taught me to be. If people will follow their heart, the world will be a little closer to Radiant Peace.

~ Summer Stone, age 9, grade 4
Walker Elementary School, Northport, Alabama (1995)

So another way to keep Radiant Peace in my world is to keep peace between my bedroom and the one next door. That would be my little brother.

~ Lauren Keen, age 13, grade 7
St. Paul Catholic School, St. Petersburg, Florida (2002)

Radiant Peace begins when I remember to kiss my mommy, daddy, grandmas and brothers. It keeps growing when I hug my friends. I share with everyone so we won't have a fight. I'm kind to my family and friends. I keep love in my heart and smiles on my face.

~ Dana de la Garza, age 6, grade 1
Freddy Gonzalez Elementary School, Edinburg, Texas (1996)

I am a Radiant Peacemaker when I compromise, share and cheer people on. I compromise when I do something I do not want to do but my brother does. I share my toys with friends. When I cheer for others it makes me feel happy.

~ David Malinoski, age 6, grade 1
Brooker Creek Elementary School, Tarpon Springs, Florida (2009)

First of all, since you have to start somewhere sharing Radiant Peace I would start in my family. If we got mad at each other, plan A would be talking. If we couldn't talk, I would say "pillow fight" just to vent anger, perfect!

~ Matt Cooper, age 9, grade 4
Weston, Florida (1996)

Radiant Peace means having a lake without ripples, a dog without fleas, a night without homework, and a dinner without lima beans. However, I would most want Radiant Peace to mean a world that is never mean.

~ Ashley Winn, age 7, grade 2
Friendship School, Coatesville, Pennsylvania (1994)

Radiant Peace begins in the family, with friends and in your thoughts, in your deeds. It brings a song to your heart, and this sound travels the whole world through. Radiant Peace is possible if we want it!

Radiant Peace Project created by children ages 8 & 9, grades 2a & 2b
Vienna, Austria (2000)

The one thing I am working very hard on is very small. It is for me and my sister to get along. It is wonderful if an 11 or 12 year old can contribute Radiant Peace to the world or even one state. One person can do the smallest things but after a while they will add up to a very large difference.

~ Nicole Hubbard, grade 5, age 11
Vance Elementary School, Vance, Alabama (1992)

One thing that I have done to achieve Radiant Peace is stop fighting with my sister by telling her I love her when we want to fight. The word "love" seem to melt hate away and this brings Radiant Peace in my world and in my home.

~ Ashley Lumberson, age 9, grade 4
Ft. Lauderdale, Florida (1996)

Radiant Peace is like the wind. You can't see it but you can feel it. It is everywhere, in the air, in our energy, and most of all in our hearts. Everyone has Radiant Peace within them. They don't always show it, but it is there. It is almost like a light in your heart which only you can choose to turn on and show. One person can make a difference when it comes to spreading Radiant Peace. I express Radiant Peace by being kind to others and by treating others the way I would want to be treated, no matter what religion, race, age, or gender. We should not judge anyone for who they are or who they want to be. Everyone should be respected and treated equally. We are all a family with Radiant Peace within us.

~ Madeleine Navilio, age 13, grade 7
Unity School, Delray Beach, Florida (2011)

I think the world would have more Radiant Peace if my brother would leave me alone when I am doing my homework.

~ Jenny Youngblood, age 9, grade 3
Vance Elementary School, Vance, Alabama (1991)

I make Radiant Peace in my life by going out to ride my bike. When I am mad at my brother, I go outside. There is no one out there and I ride my bike fast. I ride until I am not mad anymore. Then I go and play with him.

~ Alex Macon, age 7, grade 2
Broadview School, Winchester, Tennessee (1995)

Radiant Peace is making delicious palachinkies (crepes) with my Baba. When we are making food and she smiles at me, I feel like gold. Eating with my Baba makes me feel happy in my heart. That's what Radiant Peace is to me!

~ Eden Zdravko, age 7, grade 2
Brooker Creek Elementary School, Tarpon Springs, Florida (2011)

I make Radiant Peace in my heart when I help others. I help my brother when he is hurt. I make Radiant Peace in my heart when my brother thinks a favorite toy is broken and I help him make it right. When I have joy in my heart, there is joy in his.

~ David Vivian, age 8, grade 2
Holy Family Catholic School, St. Petersburg, Florida (1997)

Radiant Peace to me is helping my mom after her surgeries. I helped her get up so she could walk. I would get a blanket and something to drink when she needed it. It made me feel good.

~ Hailey Alyssa Disalvio, age 8, grade 3
Brooker Creek Elementary School, Tarpon Springs, Florida (2008)

Radiant Peace is a world sticking together as one big family.

~ Christina Maggio, age 11, grade 6
St. Paul Catholic School, St. Petersburg, Florida (2005)

I feel Radiant Peace when I'm fishing with my Dad. I think about the fish living under the water and wonder what they are doing. I also tell my Dad jokes. I smile a lot on fishing days and I tell the fish we caught, "See you at dinner!"

~ Justin Michael Dailey, age 7, grade 2
Our Lady of Hope/St. Luke School, Baltimore, Maryland (1998)

Radiant Peace is a time to love and care with your mom and dad. But do not forget your dog and your teacher.

~ Veda Loyd, age 6, grade 1
Nuestro School, Live Oak, California (1999)

Radiant Peace on earth should start with me and my sister getting along. Then everyone would be happy.

~ Abby Miller, age 6, grade 1
Walden Lake Elementary School, Plant City, Florida (2004)

Radiant Peace is how I feel when I eat cherry licorice with my grandma!

~ Jackson Palla, age 7, grade 2
Brooker Creek Elementary School, Tarpon Springs, Florida (2011)

After going through a stressful day, I find Radiant Peace inside my sister's daughter, Azuri. I treat her like she's my own daughter. When I'm out in the street people are judging me all the time, and it's stressful to live up to everyone's expectations. When I enter my sister's house I find someone that loves me, flaws and all.

I feel pressure to provide, pressure to do the right thing, pressure to make the right decision on what my next move is going to be. I feel pressure building up from late school work, so I search for Radiant Peace, and I find it inside a one-year-old's smile.

~ Ricky Hightower, age 17, grade 11
Gibbs High School, St. Petersburg, Florida (2008)

Radiant Peace is waking up in the morning and seeing your mom or dad and saying, "I am lucky to have this family."

~ Axel Troy Taylor, age 9, grade 4
Azalea Elementary School, St. Petersburg, Florida (2012)

Radiant Peace is a natural feeling inside us. Radiant Peace is when my parents and I are watching a funny movie and laugh together. Radiant Peace is to see my mother's face when I get an A on my tests. Radiant Peace is when I hug my parents.

~ Jesse Ortiz, age 5, grade K
Miami Community Charter School, Florida City, Florida (2010)

I would make more Radiant Peace in the world by being kind, sharing, and showing respect. Everyone should be doing their part. By sharing and giving my toys to others, I show kindness and Radiant Peace. I've learned this from my mom. Sharing and giving away my toys shows respect to others.

~ Alaina Seidle, age 6, grade 1
West Broward Christian School, Ft. Lauderdale, Florida (2000)

There are many different ways to make Radiant Peace in the new millennium. One way is to be more kind to other people. After all, Radiant Peace has to start with one person. Another way to bring Radiant Peace is to stop fighting with my brother and I think that would bring world peace. Remember Radiant Peace has to start with someone. If you just stand around waiting for Radiant Peace it won't happen. So why not let it start with you?

~ Neil Holloway, age 11, grade 6
St. Mark's Academy, Cocoa, Florida (1999)

I think families that show Radiant Peace should get an award.

~ Anabel Garcia, age 9, grade 4
Arnaz School, Oak View, California (1992)

Radiant Peace means that when I wake up I will get dressed and not complain about breakfast even if we are having broccoli. I will eat all of my snack, even if it kills me. I would like to make this my plan for a few days or possibly forever.

~ Aaron Mueller, age 10, grade 5
Rolling Green School, Urbandale, Iowa (1991)

I am a Radiant Peacemaker when I make a difference at home and in the community. I can walk away and ignore my brother when he fights with me. When I see a stray cat, I can feed it and try to find it a home with nice people.

~ Skylar Bodinski, age 8, grade 3
Mt. Vernon Elementary School, St. Petersburg, Florida (2009)

Radiant Peace is the love in my mom's smile!

~ Brandon White, age 6, grade 1
Crest Hill Elementary School, Casper, Wyoming (2008)

The Radiant Peace Foundation International, Inc. is an educational organization and is not religious, political or activist

My commitment to Radiant Peace in the world begins at home by not causing trouble and getting into fights with my brother. I try to do my chores cheerfully, and try not to complain when somebody else gets to do something I'm not allowed to do. Maybe just doing it in my family will not help, but if you and all your relatives and friends, and their relatives and friends, and their relatives and friends, and so on and so forth, try to peaceful to one another, soon the world will start to have more Radiant Peace.

~ Julia Cohen, grade 5
North Beach Elementary School, Miami, Florida (1991)

Three months ago my opa got very sick. When I visited him, I had a peaceful feeling in the love I have for him... Cancer is a sickness that can easily drop a strong man to his knees. My opa had lost power in his left leg. When I helped him with things he needed, it gave me peace. I gave up playing time to help him. Sometimes it's hard to wake up at night to give him a hand. Knowing that I'm doing everything I can gives me Radiant Peace.

~ Bruce Klein, age 10, grade 4
John F. Turner Elementary School, Palm Bay, Florida (1998)

Radiant Peace is what I feel in my heart every time my Nana gives me one of her special squeeze hugs. I wish my Nana could squeeze hug the whole world so everyone would feel Radiant Peace.

~ James Tassone, age 7, grade 2
Brooker Creek Elementary School, Tarpon Springs, Florida (2011)

I think Radiant Peace can mean many different things. Radiant Peace to me means: no more hunger in all countries, having harmony with other people, and togetherness all around the world.

Radiant Peace is such an important thing that everyone should have it in their lives. If we start with Radiant Peace in our homes, we will bring it into our community, and this will spread throughout our world.

~ Joani Counts, age 10, grade 5
Hearn Elementary School, Frankfort, Kentucky (1991)

6 Radiant Peace and Love

Radiant Peace is love in each one of us and the most powerful power in the world is love. Radiant Peace supports the power in all of us. It helps us grow strong. Radiant Peace is in all of us.

~ Leo Gast, age 7, grade 1
Summit-Questa Montessori School, Davie, Florida (2012)

Radiant Peace brings love to my heart and love brings joy to my life.

~ T.J. Bubar, age 9
Florida (2004)

I know Radiant Peace is in everyone. I know people around the world have Radiant Peace in them if they only look into their hearts and try.

~ Melina McGahey, age 8, grade 2
Summit-Questa Montessori School, Davie, Florida (2011)

Radiant Peace in the world can be better achieved if everyone would learn to love and live with one another. Also, don't be too rushed to enjoy the little things in life. Smiles, hugs and kind words can make anyone feel more peaceful.

~ Michael Gueno, age 10, grade 5
Shenandoah Elementary School, Baton Rouge, Louisiana (1992)

Radiant Peace is inside everyone even though it doesn't show sometimes. Radiant Peace is about love and giving. Radiant Peace means to love and to care for everyone, even your enemies.

~ Hanna Prater, age 11, grade 6
Nuestro School, Live Oak, California (2009)

I make Radiant Peace in my heart when I kiss my mom and dad and touch a butterfly.

~ Sabrina Bratsch, age 6, grade 1
John F. Turner Elementary School, Palm Bay, Florida (1999)

I make Radiant Peace when I show love for someone. When I care for maybe just one person I feel Radiant Peace inside my heart. I don't care if that somebody that I cared for isn't going to tell everyone what I did. Everything that can make you a peaceful person doesn't have to be top story news. It can be something small and simple such as helping others. Doing something so small and so simple in your eyes may be something great and large in someone else's.

~ Brittany Kelly, age 10, grade 5
Florida College Academy, Temple Terrace, Florida (2004)

Radiant Peace is love to my family, friends, teachers and the earth and the whole world.

~ Jagger Walrave, age 7, grade 1
Summit-Questa Montessori School, Davie, Florida (2010)

I learned how to find Radiant Peace in myself from my mother. She taught me when I was very young to believe in myself and to love others... I learned that we all are very different and we should accept others just the way they are and love them for their uniqueness. In loving others I learned that joy comes from it and gives me Radiant Peace in myself.

~ Amanda Saymanski, age 8, grade 3
Savanna Ridge Elementary School, Port St. Lucie, Florida (1998)

People were not created to murder, fight or treat people badly. We were put on earth for one reason and one reason only, to love one another; but we do not do that.

~ Heather Thomas, age 10, grade 4
Vance Elementary School, Vance, Alabama (1992)

Radiant Peace is loving with no strings attached.

~ Healy Dwyer, grade 8
Unity School, Delray Beach, Florida (2007)

Radiant Peace brings out the good in our hearts and souls. It is like a dove, spreading hope and joy within us. It is like a calm soothing voice telling us to love and care for others... Radiant Peace helps us to live. It helps us through the hard times.... Share the Radiant Peace within you. Help others to find their Radiant Peace. Radiant Peace is a wonderful thing.

~ Caitlin Grimes, age 10, grade 5
Wellington School, St. Petersburg, Florida (2007)

Radiant Peace is like finding a friend in a scary place. Radiant Peace is like warm sunshine on your face. Radiant Peace is love.

~ Jacob Harvey, age 8, grade 2
Brooker Creek Elementary School, Tarpon Springs, Florida (2007)

Radiant Peace is when you
love one another
Not just as a friend
But as a sister or brother

Is it found down below
Or way up above
It is really found in the center
In a heart filled with love

~ Luis Porras, age 12, grade 7
St. Timothy Parish School, Miami, Florida (2009)

We must get the message across to love and not hate. That we are all one on this super highway of life. The same air I breath today, my brothers and sisters in Africa will breath tomorrow. Also the same dust that surrounds me today will be around my fellow man in Japan tomorrow. What I can do right now is to say a prayer for our world leaders to make peace not war. I pray that I can look at my friend or someone half way around the world and see a child or an adult and see love and Radiant Peace.

~ Esbertha Lewis, age 9, grade 4
Clara Muhammad School, Miami, Florida (1996)

Radiant Peace is treating each other like a family, giving love to the world around us.

~ Alexandra Weber, age 10, grade 4
Perkins Elementary School, St. Petersburg, Florida (2007)

I create Radiant Peace when I love all the people that I know. If all the people that I love would love all the people that they know, pretty soon everybody would love everybody in the world. Radiant Peace is when I love others.

~ Brian J. Bateman, Jr., age 7, grade 1
Our Lady of Calvary School, Philadelphia, Pennsylvania (1996)

"Radiant Peace" can be described in many different ways. ...let's take a look at what the Webster's New World Dictionary has to say about the matter.

Radiant (adj.) 1. Shining brightly 2. Showing pleasure, etc.; beaming 3. Issuing from a source in or as in rays
Peace (n.) 1. Freedom from war 2. An agreement to end war 3. Law and order 4. Harmony; concord 5. Serenity or quiet

Even though these definitions may give you the idea of the sun spreading harmony and serenity around the world, I don't really think that's what Radiant Peace really means.... Life isn't about waking up in the morning with regrets. So love the people who treat you right, along with the people who don't....

Radiant Peace (n.) 1. Spreading happiness and love in an outward action 2. Having hope for yourself and for others, even when things seem to be the worst.

~ Makenzie Degenhardt, age 13, grade 7
Westlake Christian School, Palm Harbor, Florida (2009)

I make Radiant Peace in my heart when I help people. I love people. When I see someone crying I help them. I like to play with friends when they are sad. I like giving toys to people. I love to make Radiant Peace. I love the world. I can help.

~ *Lenora Carter, age 7, grade 2*
Nuestro School, Live Oak, California (1996)

Your heart is the power of Radiant Peace within you.

~ *Seth Adams, age 9, grade 4*
Lakeview Fundamental Elementary School, St. Petersburg, Florida (2008)

My parents taught me that love and patience are the keys to Radiant Peace. People like kindness. When I hear kids making fun of other people, it makes me sad. The peace has been broken. I do my best to remind my friends that it hurts people's feelings. It is important to love all things.

~ *Chandler E. Hogue, age 7, grade 2*
Brigham Academy, Winter Haven, Florida (1999)

Radiant Peace means love inside your heart that is brightened by loving and good things you do.

~ *Sydney Francis, age 7, grade 2*
St. John the Evangelist School, Pensacola, Florida (2008)

76

Radiant Peace is freedom and beams of joy.
It feels very very good in my heart and
outside of my heart too.

~ Jacob Fletcher, age 10, grade 4
PACE - Brantley Hall School, Longwood, Florida (2007)

Radiant Peace is within us all and is the best part of everyone. Radiant Peace is like a ray of light that shines in your heart. You can keep it to yourself or you can share it with others. If you share it with others, the ray of light gets stronger within you. It is like the most beautiful butterfly that you cannot wait to show to your friends. Radiant Peace helps us all to be kind and helpful to others. It is what makes us the best people we can be.

Radiant Peace is within all of our hearts. If everyone would let their Radiant Peace come out, the world would be a much better place. Everyone would be happier and there would not be as many wars.

~ Lori Lockwood, age 10, grade 5
Indian Harbour Montessori School, Indian Harbour Beach, Florida (2010)

Radiant Peace is making the world better by loving and sharing with everyone. People are loving people they don't even know.

~ Isabella Emilia Klar, age 7, grade 2
Summit-Questa Montessori School, Davie, Florida (2009)

Having a real loving concern for all mankind would help Radiant Peace. If we had a better understanding of why different people live by different standards and styles, we would be better able to get along. I think it will take a lot of cooperation. I think the most important key is togetherness.

~ Elaina Epps, age 10, grade 5
Pleasant Hill Elementary School, Oklahoma City, Oklahoma (1992)

The Radiant Peace Education Awards® are open
to all students in grades 1-12 worldwide

Radiant Peace means to be yourself, to free your heart and to give and receive love from other open hearts. When I think of Radiant Peace I see love, peace and joy connecting all of us.

~ Riley Busch, age 9, grade 4
St. Paul's School - Riverside, Jacksonville, Florida (2008)

Radiant Peace is knowing that someone in the world loves you.

~ Anthony Pumilia, grade 8
Unity School, Delray Beach, Florida (2007)

Radiant Peace is about forgiving others for hurting your feelings and forgiving yourself for what you have done wrong to them. I find Radiant Peace when I talk my worries away to someone who loves me. It feels great to know that they care about me and can help me with my hurts.

~ *Christopher Wilson, age 11, grade 5*
Apollo Elementary School, Titusville, Florida (1998)

Radiant Peace is love that flows through us. It is a warm blueberry pie that everyone can have a slice of. It is the feeling you get when someone helps you out and you just want to spread it around. So pass the pie around.

~ *Ian MacCartney, age 13, grade 8*
Westlake Christian School, Palm Harbor, Florida (2009)

What Radiant Peace means to me is non-stop love from the heart.

~ *Brianna Burke, age 8, grade 2*
Summit-Questa Montessori School, Davie, Florida (2011)

Radiant Peace is engraved in our hearts.
Radiant Peace is in all of us.

~ *Preston McDonald, age 9, grade 4*
Ridgecrest Elementary School, Largo, Florida (2009)

7 Radiant Peace and the World

I believe when one person spreads Radiant Peace, it affects your city, town and even your world. Together, with Radiant Peace, we can change the world.

~ Madison Levy, age 13, grade 8
Unity School, Delray Beach, Florida (2012)

Radiant Peace means that you can see past people's outsides, and look deep into their hearts to figure out one simple way we are all alike: We all have the power and strength to make Radiant Peace in our world.

~ Brianne Duffy, age 10, grade 4
Green Valley Elementary School, New Albany, Indiana (2000)

Radiant Peace is everyone in the world knowing the world isn't to fight about. It's for people to live on.

~ Christopher Kennedy, age 9, grade 4
J.P. Manning School, Jamaica Plain, Massachusetts (1992)

Radiant Peace is not only a feeling, but it is also an ability that can be learned and expanded. I believe that fully developing and using our capacity to spread Radiant Peace is our greatest gift to the world.

~ Mateus Falci, age 15, grade 10
American Heritage School, Plantation, Florida (2008)

Radiant Peace around the world begins with me because I control how I treat other people. Radiant Peace means more than just not fighting. Radiant Peace means being nice to people instead of fighting. Radiant Peace means forgiving people instead of fighting. Radiant Peace means helping other people not fight. I can do all of these things.

~ Brennan A. Cox, age 6, grade 1
Cross of Christ School, DeSoto, Texas (1996)

Radiant Peace is all around the world in everyone.

~ Sammy Iliff, age 9, grade 4
Perkins Elementary School, St. Petersburg, Florida (2006)

I can help the world have more Radiant Peace by treating people with honor. If I treat everybody I meet like they are special just the way they are, then everyone would not be arguing and fighting.

~ Cregg Mitchell, age 9, grade 3
Mt. Vernon Elementary School, St. Petersburg, Florida (2002)

We will not reach peace just because of the ending of wars. We must also have a deep understanding and respect for our fellow humans and living creatures. It is time to break free of war and start using a smile and a gentle helping hand and bring ever-lasting Radiant Peace into our lives.

~ Masatoshi Mochizuki, age 13, grade 8
Bay Point Middle School, St. Petersburg, Florida (2000)

How can I bring Radiant Peace to the world? Sounds to me like a huge undertaking. Would I have to become a governmental leader or some world-renowned peacemaker? Surely isn't simple, is it? I mean, how could a smile, so simple an idea, make a difference for someone? Or volunteering to help feed homeless people, could that make a difference in the world? It may not be a headline and news breaking difference, but it may be a difference to someone who is sad and in need of a smile, or someone who is hungry and wants food. Right now if you turned to the person next to you and smiled, you could make a difference in their world. And who knows, that smile may carry on to someone halfway across the world. So you don't need anything flashy, great governmental powers, or money. I can bring Radiant Peace to the world.

~ Ryan Spears, age 14, grade 8
St. Paul Catholic School, St. Petersburg, Florida (2002)

Radiant Peace should be contagious like a cold!

~ Aubrey Court, age 12, grade 7
Laurel Nokomis School, Nokomis, Florida (2005)

There are many people who have unhappy lives, bitter feelings and anger stored inside of them. Only when they can find Radiant Peace in their hearts can we have real peace around the world.

~ Michael Citron, age 9, grade 4
Ojus Elementary School, North Miami Beach, Florida (1991)

Radiant Peace is helping one another regardless of race or religion. Radiant Peace is also being friends with people no matter what differences you have. Radiant Peace for the world is a lot like everything else in life. Wishing will only get you half way. We all have to work together for the goal of Radiant Peace. We can help get closer to that goal by accepting one another, being willing to compromise and acknowledging each other's good qualities. That is how we can all work together to find Radiant Peace within ourselves and in the world.

~ Nickolas Murray, age 14, grade 8
Nuestro School, Live Oak, California (2012)

The best part about sharing Radiant Peace is that you are not just helping one person; instead it is like a chain reaction, endless! We can all make a difference in the lives of people of the world, and it all starts with you expressing Radiant Peace!

~ Haley Rinderle, age 13, grade 7
Westlake Christian School, Palm Harbor, Florida (2009)

Radiant Peace is like making lasagna with all the souls in the world. The homeless people, children and the not homeless people come together and form Radiant Peace. It is the sweetest thing you could do.

~ Tyler Jackson, age 6, grade 1
Wellington School, St. Petersburg, Florida (2006)

Radiant Peace is like a river because a river joins other bodies of water to become one. When we live together being kind and nice to each other Radiant Peace gives us a chance to become one.

~ Leslie Ellis, age 10, grade 5
Brighton Elementary School, Brighton, Tennessee (1991)

I imagine Radiant Peace as a mother who holds in her arms children from the whole world.

~ Peristeri, age 8
Bucharest, Romania (1999)

I help the world have Radiant Peace by helping people, respecting people, and treating people as I want to be treated. If this world was full of Radiant Peace, you would not have to worry hardly about anything going wrong in this world. My parents would not have to worry about anything happening to me if they send me to the store... I wish that I had a vacuum cleaner that could suck up all the wrong things that were done in this world.

~ Precious Willis, age 10, grade 4
Jacksonville, Florida (1995)

Radiant Peace should spread all around the world and last forever.

~ J.T. Hadley, age 9, grade 4
Perkins Elementary School, St. Petersburg, Florida (2006)

I can make more Radiant Peace in the world by stopping fights, working together, and being kind. It hurts other people when you are mean and push them around. I also don't judge people and I talk out problems with my friends. If we love ourselves and respect others, the world will have more Radiant Peace.

~ Miranda Marra-Owen, age 7, grade 2
Spruce Creek Elementary School, Port Orange, Florida (2001)

The world has wars and people have fights. In a way they're the same. Because of wars the world can fall, because of fights I can fall. The world needs Radiant Peace and I can help easily. So can everyone else.

~ Andrew Faubel, age 10, grade 5
Miami, Florida (1996)

Radiant Peace is in my heart all the time. It is there when I help my friends and other people. Helping people makes you special.

~ Emely Casada, age 8, grade 3
The Learning Center, Tampa, Florida (2009)

Radiant Peace is when one person's love and happiness spreads to someone else, and then that person spreads it and so on. Think of Radiant Peace as radiation in science. The scientific term is a type of heat transfer. You can't see it, but you can feel it. You can't see Radiant Peace, but you can definitely feel it. It makes you feel warm and good inside.

~ Nolin Bohon, age 11, grade 6
Collierville Middle School, Collierville, Tennessee (2012)

There are many ways I express Radiant Peace in my life, one of which is just making someone feel better. If someone is sad, if someone made fun of them or if they aren't having a good day you could make them feel better by being nice to them. Another way to express Radiant Peace is by spreading it through the hearts of everyone on the planet. If you express Radiant Peace then someone else will see you expressing Radiant Peace and get inspired to do so as well. As this process goes on it will spread all around the world. So go out and express Radiant Peace in your life, and who knows? Maybe you'll change the world!

~ Garrett Wilkinson, age 12, grade 6
St. Paul Catholic School, St. Petersburg, Florida (2010)

**If I were President we would have
a Radiant Peace parade ten times a year!**

~ Courtney Anderson, age 9, grade 4
Pease Elementary School, Austin, Texas (1992)

Radiant Peace in the world to me, a ten year old, means the whole world can get along with each other no matter what color or custom. People act blind because of their lack of knowledge of others and their customs. We are really the same. We started a bad habit of settling our problems with war.

~ Andrea Kartley, age 10, grade 5
Greenview Upper Elementary School, South Euclid, Ohio (1991)

87

I share Radiant Peace when I pull someone out of their sadness and into the light. Radiant Peace is in everyone and when you unleash yours and share it with someone you unleash theirs too. The more you share Radiant Peace the better the world becomes.

~ Simon Akhnoukh, age 9, grade 4
Ridgecrest Elementary School, Largo, Florida (2007)

I'm a Radiant Peacemaker when I help people up when they fall playing games and when I play fair.

~ Sean Plunkett, age 7, grade 2
Summit-Questa Montessori School, Davie, Florida (2009)

I believe there is a Radiant Peace that lingers within each and every person. It's the steady beat of a heart, birds singing at sunrise, and maybe even a car ride with all the windows down singing loud enough for the world to hear. I also believe that everyone is capable of Radiant Peace. Radiant Peace is within the individual, the people, and the world.

Embracing someone as a person can be especially hard for some people. It may be coming to terms with your mistakes and failures, differences or a new perspective of the world. What matters is that at the end of the day one can find what is truly important in a quiet place called the heart.

Nevertheless, how can we as people obtain peace, not having grasped and mastered it ourselves. Once a person has done so, we can all move forward obtaining peace with one another....

...Whether or not we choose to believe, embrace, or achieve our Radiant Peace is up to us as individuals. Once we do we can all be peaceful together in one radiantly peaceful world.

~ Andrea Stojanovic, age 17, grade 11
Countryside High School, Clearwater, Florida (2011)

If I were President, I would make a game that everyone would want to play. I'd call the game "World of Radiant Peace." People would play the game day and night at work and at home. The goal would be to love other people. The rules would be:

- Help someone at least once a day
- Take someone home every week who is homeless and give them care
- Feed someone who is hungry until they are full
- Share at least once a day
- Get to know someone who is different from you
- Smile and laugh as much as you can

I would teach this game to our country first. Then I would send messengers to all countries to teach them how to play the game. Soon all people around the whole world would play the game because it makes you feel so good inside! Then we would truly have a world of Radiant Peace.

~ Grant Jolly, age 9, grade 4
Judson School, Phoenix, Arizona (1994)

If I were President, to promote Radiant Peace in the world, first of all I would be a person of Radiant Peace myself. How many people does it take to make Radiant Peace? As President, I would declare every day a Radiant Peace day, and hope this Radiant Peace would spread all around the world, one person at a time.

~ Blakely Smith, age 9, grade 4
Maude Saunders Elementary School, DeFuniak Springs, Florida (1994)

Maybe if humans acted as peaceful as my fish it could change the world. . .My fish get along well in a small area, and we could learn from that.

~ *Shane, age 8, grade 2*
Virginia A. Boone Highland Oaks Elementary School, Miami, Florida (1998)

I can help to achieve Radiant Peace in the world by keeping an open mind. As a small boy in the streets of Harlem, New York, I can't hardly imagine a world with Radiant Peace. It appears to me that small people seem to be the only ones thinking about Radiant Peace. So I decided that the best thing I can do for Radiant Peace in the world is to keep an open mind. That's not an easy task in the day of a small boy like me. In the morning my dad always sounds like a grizzly bear. Then, my-oh-my; the streets, the teachers, the class, "oops", there goes my open mind. It's like a time-clock! I can always reset it and start my Radiant Peace process all over again.

~ *Ronald DeCosta, age 9, grade 4*
P.S. 108, New York, New York (1996)

People say they want Radiant Peace in the world. It could eventually happen. It starts one person at a time. The only person you can really change is yourself. Once you work on yourself, it makes it easier to help others.

~ *Lindsey Nicola, age 14, grade 8*
Westlake Christian School, Palm Harbor, Florida (2009)

90

Radiant Peace is me, you, and the world. Radiant Peace is not for one, but for all. Radiant Peace cannot be held in your hand, but in your heart. Radiant Peace is for all.

~ Kelcey Ross, age 9, grade 4
Ridgecrest Elementary School, Largo, Florida (2009)

Radiant Peace in the world can be achieved through many different ways. In many ways my commitment is very small, compared to what the leaders of nations could quickly do to maintain world peace... My commitment, although small, might contribute to something big together with other commitments from the children of the world. I should start in my house. I can help my parents, think before getting upset with my brother and sister, be kind to the pets and other animals, enjoy and respect all the beautiful things that God and nature have given us.

I can also take advantage of the fact that I live in the most wonderful country in the world, where education is a right and learn as much as I can. Maybe someday I can help others learn and better themselves because I would love to be a teacher. In my school and my community, I can be a friend to whoever wants my friendship and love everybody in this world.

~ Ana Abaunza, grade 3
Royal Green Elementary School, Miami, Florida (1991)

Radiant Peace is something to trust, something to hold hands for and something for the world to share. I believe Radiant Peace goes around the world like an angel's song or the rays of the sun. Radiant Peace is love and happiness.

~ Melina McGahey, age 8, grade 2
Summit-Questa Montessori School, Davie, Florida (2012)

This recipe for Radiant Peace, I hope you will enjoy.

Everyone should make it, man, woman, girl, or boy.

Just get a baking pan the size of your heart.

You don't preheat the oven so you should be able to start.

Spread some love on the bottom of the pan, just about an inch.

Sprinkle on some loving smiles, just a pinch.

Add 5 ounces of sharing and take out all hatred and hurt.

Now, stir in a world of people that are not mean or curt.

Put in 16 teaspoons of caring, animals, flowers and fun and presto a creation that is #1!

The ingredients in this recipe are words that explain how I feel about beautiful Radiant Peace! Now, go share your masterpiece meal!

~ Kristen Lynne Soltis, age 9, grade 4
Blankner Elementary School, Orlando, Florida (1993)

We should always communicate with new people.
Always talk to people no matter what color they are.
Always treat people and the earth with respect.

~ Alexis Dynneson, age 10, grade 5
Brorson School, Sidney, Montana (2006)

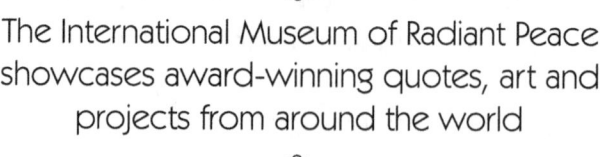

The International Museum of Radiant Peace
showcases award-winning quotes, art and
projects from around the world

A Recipe for Radiant Peace in the World
Serves: All human kind

Ingredients: A large pan the size of your soul, love, caring hands, kisses, tea spoon, young kids with smiles from ear to ear, sifter, hugs, flowers, heart and cake platter.

Directions: Get a large pan the size of your soul. Now let's begin! Spread some love on the bottom of the pan about 1 inch thick. Pat it down with caring hands. Sprinkle on kisses just a bit. Add 12 kids playing with a smile from ear to ear. Sift out all the war and hate. Now add two ounces of hugs and flowers. Now bake it in your heart. This is what I would do for Radiant Peace. Don't you think this is the best cake you ever had.

~ Ryan L. Stephens, age 10, grade 4
Huntsville Elementary School, Huntsville, Texas (1994)

When I think of Radiant Peace, I feel fearless and happy. It is like the world is fulled with love and peace. Radiant Peace also makes me feel like I have the whole world in my hands.

~ Leah Bellamy, age 12, grade 5
McMullen Booth Elementary School, Clearwater, Florida (2009)

Radiant Peace is fantastic!

~ Ufuk S., grade 4
Berlin, Germany (2002)

93

8 Radiant Peace: Exploring Our Diversity

It doesn't matter how old or young you are,
Radiant Peace is in your heart; making you shine
by just being you.

~ Mason A. Lively, grade 5
Indian Harbour Montessori School, Indian Harbour Beach, Florida (2010)

Radiant Peace, to me, is strong love and care for people, animals and plants that make the world a better place. Radiant Peace brings everyone closer together with friendship no matter what differences they have.

~ Robby Leggat, age 8, grade 3
Castaic Elementary School, Castaic, California (2012)

Radiant Peace on earth is loving everyone for who they are on the inside, not for who they are on the outside.

~ Juliane Nylund, age 13, grade 8
Westlake Christian School, Palm Harbor, Florida (2004)

Radiant Peace is what holds you and I together. Radiant Peace holds many secrets. It is in everybody whether or not you are black, white, red or yellow. Radiant Peace - what a wonderful choice!!

~ April Summers, age 10, grade 5
Dryden Elementary School, Dryden, Michigan (1991)

It doesn't matter who is small. It doesn't matter who is big. Radiant Peace is about caring and sending happiness feelings across the world.

~ *Shrey Deshmukh, age 7, grade 2*
Brooker Creek Elementary School, Tarpon Springs, Florida (2008)

Radiant Peace is everyone shining and being themselves without being judged.

~ *Morgan R., age 11, grade 6*
Wellington School, St. Petersburg, Florida (2007)

Radiant Peace is someone opening their heart to forgive. Radiant Peace is someone loving and giving to another. Radiant Peace is a light that shines brightly from our hearts and radiates into the hearts and lives of those around us. Radiant Peace is more valuable than all the riches in the world. Radiant Peace helps the world come together as one, by unlocking the boundaries of race, culture and differences among each other.

~ *Michael Deib, age 8, grade 3*
Brooker Creek Elementary School, Tarpon Springs, Florida (2011)

Radiant Peace starts within our soul, and once we find it, a chain reaction winds through our bodies into our hearts and minds. The world would be free of prejudice and warfare if we chose to light the candle of Radiant Peace that exists in all of us.

~ *Kayleigh, age 12, grade 7*
Tequesta Trace Middle School, Weston, Florida (1998)

To me Radiant Peace means many different things. Radiant Peace is being able to travel to different places and countries without having to worry about being harmed because of the way I look or the country I may be from. Radiant Peace is being able to get along with your family and friends and to feel safe in your own home. Radiant Peace is when people of the world realize that we all live on the same planet, breathing the same air and drinking the same water. When the sun comes out each day it shines on everyone, not just blacks one day, whites one day and yet browns or yellows another day.

~ Stephanie Najor, age 10, grade 5
Deer Canyon Elementary School, San Diego, California (1992)

Radiant Peace is making friends and helping others. It doesn't matter if we have different colored skin or have different religions. We are all human.

~ Julia Parra, age 9, grade 3
Summit-Questa Montessori School, Davie, Florida (2012)

To me, Radiant Peace is when I can wear whatever I want and no one will judge me. It's when I can be whatever size I want and not worry about others' comments. It's when I can be 16 years old and still listen to nursery rhymes if I want to. It's when I can be best friends with someone who's the complete opposite to me. It's when child labor is just a thing in the past. It's when I can't wait for tomorrow to come. It's when living actually feels like being alive . . . .

~ Mona Omar, age 15, grade 10
Dar El Tarbiah American School, Cairo, Egypt (2010)

Radiant Peace is including everyone even if you don't like them. Everyone is different in one way or another. You should not just be friends with people who are like you because you could learn new things from the people who are different. A lot of wars have started because people cannot accept other people's differences. Radiant Peace is showing and giving peace to the world. It is not judging people on how they look or act. It is finding the best in everybody.

~ Justina John, age 9, grade 4
Ridgecrest Elementary School, Largo, Florida (2012)

Radiant Peace is energy within the soul that lets a person be themselves without discrimination. Radiant Peace is harmless. It helps the world to be a better place for the next generation and beyond.

~ Ray Lisle, age 11, grade 6
PACE - Brantley Hall School, Longwood, Florida (2007)

I know that having more Radiant Peace everywhere will be hard, because we all have different beliefs. I think that it's important for us to help our neighbors if they are in need, no matter what they believe. If we take time to show some interest in positive things, we may not have so much conflict. I don't agree with people doing drugs, committing crimes, or war because a lot of innocent people get hurt. I think it is important for us to solve some of the problems in our world, but first I think we have to start by spreading Radiant Peace in our homes and communities.

~ Raven Dunn, age 10, grade 5
Woodland Forrest Elementary School, Tuscaloosa, Alabama (2002)

I understand Radiant Peace when I make friends with children of different nations or of different religions. When I first made friends with a boy of another religion I couldn't believe that it was possible to become friends with your enemy. But later we became good friends. So I understand that it is important to be a real human with all human qualities. It doesn't matter where you are from and what's your religion.

~ Abrahamyan Sahak, age 15
Gyumri, Armenia (2004)

Radiant Peace to me means not to be judged because you look and act different. No matter how you look at it, they're still humans as you and I. Look at Radiant Peace as a basketball game, but none the less the most important game of life. Time's running out. Do you want to be a hero for Radiant Peace? I ask the question again, do you want to be a hero or a zero? The choice is yours.

~ Terrence Payne, age 10, grade 5
Brighton Elementary School, Brighton, Tennessee (1993)

Radiant Peace is the master key that opens the gate to happiness. It leads us to a life of possibilities. Radiant Peace is always where love dwells. It is also where people connect to each other and become united.

~ Milaida Alvarez, age 15, grade 8
Miami Community Charter School, Florida City, Florida (2012)

I make Radiant Peace when I meet someone new and we become friends. I make Radiant Peace when I learn about people around the world. No matter where they live, they are just like you and me. Most of all, I make Radiant Peace when I am thoughtful of others.

~ Joshua Keels, age 6, grade 1
Apollo Elementary School, Titusville, Florida (1999)

To me, Radiant Peace is something that comes from the inside. When you are at peace with yourself, you can be free to be peaceful towards others. When you are at peace with yourself, it means caring and loving. It also means appreciating and accepting yourself and other people.

Radiant Peace means joy, and hope of life. Radiant Peace isn't always easy. Sometimes it's difficult, but it's a goal we must each try for....

Radiant Peace means respecting ourselves and respecting others, even if they are different from us or disagree with us. If you feel at peace with yourself, you can act peacefully no matter what happens, and that is how Radiant Peace can be created.

~ Leila Mohr, age 9, grade 4
Marquette Elementary School, Madison, Wisconsin (1993)

Radiant Peace is like shaking hands with someone different and you get to shake away all the fears.

~ Eleazar Dunbar, age 8, grade 3
Homeschool, Chicago, Illinois (2010)

I believe that Radiant Peace starts in everybodies hearts. When people learn to accept each others differences, then the world will be in Radiant Peace. This is my wish for the whole world.

~ Matthew Dugan, age 7, grade 2
Athenian Academy, Dunedin, Florida (2002)

I can't tell you what an adult's perspective is on "Radiant Peace", but I can tell you from the eyes of an eight-year-old kid. Radiant Peace is within everyone's reach. It doesn't matter what skin color you have or what religion you believe in. It doesn't matter if you're smarter or more athletic. It doesn't matter what you look like or what kind of clothes you wear.

Radiant Peace shines outward like light and heat from the sun. It's about being kind, thoughtful, loyal, generous, and respectful to others with no strings attached. It's also about happily accepting that people are all different. Some of my best friends are from different cultures and religions, but that doesn't change the way we think about each other. Our attitudes and behaviors affect everyone around us.... If we are all thoughtful about how we treat others, Radiant Peace would shine like the sun all over the world.

~ Jake Hildreth, age 8, grade 3
Castaic Elementary School, Castaic, California (2010)

Radiant Peace to me means that everyone can be who they want to be, and are able to express themselves without having to worry about being rejected. Radiant Peace is about accepting everyone for who they are; it's not about cliques and discrimination.

~ Erin Johnson, age 14, grade 8
Pinellas Preparatory Academy, Largo, Florida (2012)

Radiant Peace means to have peace inside of you that shows on the outside too. By showing and sharing this peace you are able to meet new people and make new friends no matter who they are or where they come from. That is what Radiant Peace means to me.

~ Mariella Broyles, grade 4
Summit-Questa Montessori School, Davie, Florida (2008)

Radiant Peace is when no matter what shape or color a person is, you can still be friends.

~ Joshua J. Estremera, grade 4
Pinellas Central Elementary School, Pinellas Park, Florida

9 What I would say about Radiant Peace to a child in another country....

If I talked to a child in another country about Radiant Peace I would say, if you and I were friends and we got a friend and they got a friend and so on, the whole world would be in Radiant Peace.

~ Danielle Rodriguez, age 6, grade 1
Walden Lake Elementary School, Plant City, Florida (2002)

Radiant Peace means understanding with another person. It means communicating. If we have these things there would be less fighting in the world. There would be more happiness. If I met another child I would say we need to understand our differences from each other. We need to talk and understand each other's feelings and thoughts. Then we could be friends.

~ Corey D'Angelo, age 7, grade 2
Perkins Elementary School, St. Petersburg, Florida (2002)

I would tell a child from another country that I would like to see Radiant Peace in the world. I think if we knew more about each other there might be Radiant Peace. I would ask him how he lives and tell him about me. Understanding each other will help make Radiant Peace in the world.

~ Rebecca Karttunen, age 8, grade 3
Christ Lutheran School, Cape Coral, Florida (2002)

If I talked with a child from another country about Radiant Peace I would start with love. Love is the center of Radiant Peace, the friendship love, the real love, the understanding love. I would tell them to create Radiant Peace you must always try to come to an agreement and to understand the other person's need, yet don't forget your own. I would tell them always to try to create Radiant Peace because Radiant Peace is the universal answer to harmony, love and caring for each other and the world. They will understand Radiant Peace after this.

~ Nimmerta Sangera, age 12, grade 7
Nuestro School, Live Oak, California (2002)

I would tell them that Radiant Peace brings happiness, gentleness, and friendship between countries. The best feeling in the world is to have Radiant Peace.

~ Cristina Salazar, age 11, grade 5
St. Timothy Parish School, Miami, Florida (2002)

... I will tell them that it doesn't matter what is on the outside, it matters what is on the inside.

~ Melinda Petrimoulx, age 9
Tampa, Florida (1996)

I would tell a child that I would like to be his friend. I would also tell him about America, and ask him questions about his country. I would tell him that the more we know about each other, the better chance we have of living peacefully.

~ Tyler Langbauer, age 8, grade 3
Christ Lutheran School, Cape Coral, Florida (2002)

To achieve Radiant Peace we all have to work together and support one another. We can't get mad over silly things and must make an effort to try to be kind. To live a balanced life we all need Radiant Peace, it is the foundation for happiness.

~ Diana Sakal, age 14, grade 8
All Saints Catholic School, Sunrise, Florida (2002)

I would talk to kids from other countries just like I talk to my friends. Just because they are from a different country, you don't have to treat them different... I would ask them what Radiant Peace means to them. Then I would listen to what they have to say about Radiant Peace. Then I would ask them to play basketball with me. If they don't know how to play, I would teach them.

~ Kenneth Larsen, age 13, grade 7
Nuestro School, Live Oak, California (2005)

To bring Radiant Peace into the world, we need to have harmony among each other. We should have peace with each other as friends do. When you are with a person you dislike, it is very important to show Radiant Peace in your communication. Many people made changes in the world to make it peaceful for all of us. We need to change our world from war to peace. What the world needs now is love, love, love.

~ Victoria Chavarria, age 11, grade 5
William B. Travis Elementary School, Corpus Christ, Texas (2002)

If I were talking to children in another country I would say Radiant Peace is a way of life. Radiant Peace is when two different sides of people get along in harmony. Radiant Peace is spiritual and verbal. It's more than not fighting. Radiant Peace comes from the heart. But the problem is that in this world where people are selfish and greedy, it's almost impossible to have world peace. Radiant Peace is when everyone of all the races can come together in unity.

~ Karina De La Peña, age 12, grade 7
St. Timothy Parish School, Miami, Florida (2002)

I would say that we make Radiant Peace when we do not make fun of other people. I accept other people even if they are different than me.

~ Mayra Perez, age 7, grade 1
Linwood Elementary School, Oklahoma City, Oklahoma (1999)

I want to help make Radiant Peace in the world. I try every day to be a better person. Hopefully, I can be a good example for someone. When I come across someone who seems unhappy or having a bad day I try to show kindness and a friendly attitude towards them. A kind word can really make a difference. I always try to offer a helping hand to people around me. In our world there is prejudice and anger towards different races and religions. I try to look at just the person and not the color of their skin or their religious beliefs. I simply try to get along with everyone. I feel we are all different and special in our own way. I hope by caring for my fellow man I contribute to making a world with more Radiant Peace for us all to live in.

~ Brandon Sparks, age 11, grade 5
Woodland Forrest Elementary School, Tuscaloosa, Alabama (2003)

I will tell them Radiant Peace is an act of kindness. By bringing happiness to others, you are making a strong connection of Radiant Peace. I can help create this. It might be that special touch, or those considerate words that really make a difference in someone's life. I can also make a difference by understanding others, their culture, and way of life. "Small acts can really make a big difference."

By making that special connection, I am taking small steps towards understanding different points of view. If every person on earth did this, we could bring about Radiant Peace in our world. If we showed respect to each other, the world would be a better place to live in. We would have Radiant Peace in our hearts and Radiant Peace on earth.

~ Romy Kalvaria, age 12, grade 6
Indialantic Elementary School, Indialantic, Florida (1997)

This is what I would say... Radiant Peace is being able to live with people that aren't like you. Radiant Peace is when people of different religions and backgrounds come together. Radiant Peace is knowing that someone loves you and you love someone. Radiant Peace is knowing that you can be friends with whomever you want to be. Radiant Peace is living your life the way you want to live it. Radiant Peace is when you see someone struggling and help them. We are all a part of this world, and we should make the best of it. Not everyone has discovered Radiant Peace yet, but if you have read this, we are one step forward then we were before.

~ Catherine Robertson, age 10, grade 4
St. Mark's Academy, Cocoa, Florida (2002)

I would begin by explaining Radiant Peace was loving, caring, and sharing. Having love for another person is Radiant Peace. Love is a powerful thing. Caring is also in Radiant Peace, everybody caring about what you have to say, caring about people with sickness and disease, your fellow men caring for you. Caring is what my country needs. Sharing is also important, sharing dreams, thoughts, and love for one another, sharing happiness and fun. You can even share a piece of your mind. Radiant Peace is incomplete without sharing. That is what Radiant Peace is to me. Radiant Peace is the best thing in the world. Radiant Peace is just a glorious thing.

~ Kyle Phillips, age 10, grade 5
Walker Elementary School, Northport, Alabama (2002)

10 Radiant Peace and Animals

Animals have many unique ways that bring us Radiant Peace. When dogs sense that we are sad or down, they might simply just sit at our side or jump in our lap as a way of saying "I love you," or "I'm here for you.."... I think that if people in today's world had the kind of compassion that animals have for us, the world would be full of many Radiant Peacemakers.

~ Laurie Bell, age 14, grade 8
Chalybeate School, Walnut, Mississippi (2012)

I share Radiant Peace with animals by treating them nicely. Sometimes they don't listen just like children but you don't hurt them. They take it to heart just like people do.

~ Johnnie Evans, age 11, grade 3
Mt. Vernon Elementary School, St. Petersburg, Florida (2008)

Radiant Peace to me is cuddling with my cats.

~ Sage Halpern, age 8, grade 2
Summit-Questa Montessori School, Davie, Florida (2010)

My way of sharing Radiant Peace is by taking care of my own animals. I have two dogs, a bird and a rabbit. The love I give them is from deep in my heart and is a natural love for them.

~ Carmen D. Brune, age 7, grade 2
Our Lady of Hope/St. Luke School, Baltimore, Maryland (2008)

I find Radiant Peace in myself when I'm with animals. Animals bring me comfort and I feel I bring comfort and happiness to them too. The animals who make me particularly happy are my cat Diamond and my Grandma's cat Jake... I guess it's their unconditional love and tail wagging welcomes that make me find Radiant Peace in myself. They love me for who I am.

~ *Alicia Canessa, age 11, grade 5*
Brooker Elementary School, Brandon, Florida (1999)

How I share Radiant Peace with animals is to pet them, play with them, sleep with them and be nice to them. You can also kiss them and hug them softly.

~ *Gracyn Lindborg, age 8, grade 2*
Lake Eola Charter School, Orlando, Florida (2008)

While trying to decide how to write my Radiant Peace report, I sat watching the newest member of my family, a three-year-old miniature dachshund named Buddy, nuzzle his way into a blanket on the couch. It came to me that Radiant Peace can be something as simple as a comfy crocheted blanket, a pillow to lie on or a lap to snuggle in. My dogs love to listen to stories at bedtime or sit on my lap while I watch TV at night. I believe that by being a responsible pet owner, I show my family, friends and my pets Radiant Peace.

~ *Tara Crowhurst, age 13, grade 7*
Nuestro School, Live Oak, California (2012)

Radiant Peace is when I wake up in the morning and hug each of my dogs. This makes them happy. If I woke up and started yelling at my dogs, they would soon be snarling at each other. Animals and people are a lot alike because they both have the same feelings. If people are nice to each other every morning then everyone might be very happy all day and kids would not fight and teachers would not be grouchy.

~ *Arthur McCoy, age 9, grade 4*
J.P. Manning School, Jamaica Plain, Massachusetts (1992)

When I am watching any living thing through binoculars out my window I find Radiant Peace in myself. I watch birds fly down for food, and squirrels run across the telephone lines with nuts and food. Sometimes I see a turtle in the ditch across the street.

~ *John, age 11, grade 6*
Harbor City Elementary School, Melbourne, Florida (1998)

Radiant Peace is watching my kittens play with each other and my fish swimming. Radiant Peace is laying on my bed resting with the wind blowing on me as I watch the sun.

~ *Laci Youngblood, age 7, grade 2*
Vance Elementary School, Vance Alabama (1994)

I share Radiant Peace with animals. I helped a dog. I gave food to the dog and the dog was happy. He wagged his tail. I felt happy. I hugged him. He licked me. This is the way to share Radiant Peace.

~ *Jana Pesten, age 6, grade 1*
Anglo-American School of St. Petersburg, Russia (2008)

I make Radiant Peace when I care for my family. Hugging Mom and Dad makes me feel calm and peaceful. I also make Radiant Peace when I care for my horse Merlin. I feed her carrots and bathe her. Then I go for a ride.

~ Harley Stiles, age 6, grade 1
J. Allen Axson Montessori School, Jacksonville, Florida (1999)

What Radiant Peace means to me is people being like a herd of cows grazing peacefully, not charging or hurting each other. Just eating and mooing among themselves. No killings or dangers of getting hurt by the others, just walking along and resting sometimes. But like I said before, they don't hurt each other. This is what Radiant Peace means to me.

~ Jon Hall, age 10, grade 4
Green Valley Elementary School, North Richland Hills, Texas (1993)

I love my cat, Ella. She just had five tiny kittens. Watching Ella find a safe, warm place for her kittens to be born was very interesting. I love watching how Ella takes care of them and protects them. Parents that love their children make my heart feel Radiant Peace.

~ Sydney Carter, age 8, grade 2
Chalybeate School, Walnut, Mississippi (2012)

I have a new gray little dog named Bailey. Radiant Peace is how I feel when I think about Bailey. I feel so helpful because I rescued her from the shelter.

~ August J. Papes, age 8, grade 2
Brooker Creek Elementary, Tarpon Springs, Florida (2010)

I am a Radiant Peacemaker when I draw. First, art is like Radiant Peace to me. I like to draw things like doves, rabbits, fish, dogs, colts and chickens. Second, being kind to animals is Radiant Peace. I will pet them, scratch them on their ears. I will also care for them. I am a Radiant Peacemaker.

~ Grace Lundberg, age 8, grade 3
Nuestro School, Live Oak, California (2012)

Radiant Peace is like a watchful bird being set free from inside your heart. Every time you help a person or animal you feel Radiant Peace fluttering from your heart.

~ Ashley Zhou, age 9, grade 4
Ridgecrest Elementary School, Largo, Florida (2006)

The two ways that I can help make Radiant Peace in the new millennium are by volunteering to help animals and helping people to get along... I think that if more people volunteer for different things whether it is to help people or animals and also if we could just see that being different and thinking different is actually good. We may learn something from someone else if we only just try.

~ Megan E. Grover, age 9, grade 3
Apollo Elementary School, Titusville, Florida (1999)

Radiant Peace is spread when people help animals and animals help people. Animals are like people too, and need to be loved and cared for. Animals bring us love in our hearts, beauty in our life, and provide company to us. We can share Radiant Peace with our pets. If you have a dog for your pet, the Radiant Peace you have in your heart is shared with them by caring for them. We hug and kiss our dogs. We feed them when they are hungry. We are always by their side if they are hurt. Dogs give us Radiant Peace too. They fill our hearts with love and keep people company when they are lonely. Animals can even bring us laughter. This is the Radiant Peace that animals can bring in our lives.

~ Saudia Jones, age 8, grade 3
Castaic Elementary School, Castaic, California (2011)

Radiant Peace to me is when I have respect for my dogs at home. I love them, I bathe them and I take them for walks and give them a good home to live in. My dogs, Harley, the English bulldog, and Buddy, a Pembroke Welsh Corgi are a big part of my family. They make loveable companions because like Radiant Peace they always show love to their owners.

~ Anthony Cruz, age 10, grade 5
Page Private School, Sanford, Florida (2011)

11 Radiant Peace and Nature

I listen to nature and I hear her message. She says respect, love, and cherish everything. She says that I can start at home, school, and play. Then maybe like the rays of the sun that bring warmth to the earth, I can spread rays of Radiant Peace.

~ Dina Haines, age 11, grade 5
Hopatcong, New Jersey (1995)

I find Radiant Peace in myself by going fishing. It is just so quiet. You can just think about things more. You hear waves gently crash against the bank. The wind blows so peacefully through the tops of the trees. That is one way I find Radiant Peace in myself.

~ Andrew, age 11, grade 6
Vance Elementary School, Vance, Alabama (1998)

Radiant Peace is like a seed. Give it a little love and care and it will grow into a giant tree and spread its own seeds of Radiant Peace. We need to work together to achieve Radiant Peace. It isn't something that just happens.

~ Derek Colletti, age 10, grade 6
Our Lady of Hope/St. Luke School, Baltimore, Maryland (1996)

Radiant Peace is the breeze that blows by on a summer night. Radiant Peace is the blooming of new life. Radiant Peace is nature; it is all around us.

~ Erin McEntegart, age 12, grade 6
St. Paul Catholic School, St. Petersburg, Florida (2004)

I find Radiant Peace in myself by looking up at the night sky. It's just so cool looking at a big area full of stars.

~ Brendan, age 11, grade 6
Roosevelt Elementary School, Cocoa Beach, Florida (1998)

Radiant Peace is the quietness around you on a spring day in the middle of a meadow full of daisies, birds, and butterflies. Radiant Peace is the grace of smelling a rose, of acting kindly, of caring for another. I think Radiant Peace is the love you share with everyone.

~ Jessica Devine, age 9, grade 4
Sarasota, Florida (1995)

Radiant Peace is like a flower growing. As it blooms, it sprouts leaves of joy and petals of happiness.

~ Christina Combs, age 8, grade 3
St. Mark's Academy, Cocoa, Florida (2007)

Radiant Peace to me is listening to the ocean waves move and hearing them crash against the shore. Waves come and go and this helps me understand. These waves are like life's problems. They come and they go. They help me be peaceful within myself. Waves are like big and small problems. They come to shore and they help me clear my thoughts. Radiant Peace is as deep and wide as the ocean. This all helps me understand and clear my mind and thoughts of all the problems. The ocean calms me and allows me to find Radiant Peace.

~ Natalie Alvarez, age 13, grade 8
Gettysburg Academy of Miami, Miami, Florida (1998)

I find Radiant Peace when I am outside in the cool breeze of the wind. The breeze rustles through my shiny black hair and brushes up against my body with a peaceful sway.

~ Jacinta Zhané Kimbrough, age 7, grade 2
St. Mark's Academy, Cocoa, Florida (2002)

The way I find Radiant Peace in myself is when I ride my horse and look at all the country, smell the flowers, see the hills and remember all these things.

~ Sara McMillen, age 9, grade 3
Brorson School, Sidney, Montana (1998)

I find Radiant Peace through the simple things in life, such as the warmth of the sun on a summer day, the sound of rain, watching the clouds change into their positions and anticipating what shape they might make.

~ Alexandra, age 10, grade 5
Woodland Forrest Elementary School, Tuscaloosa, Alabama (1998)

Radiant Peace is when rainbows come out after a rain storm.

~ Olivia Guido, age 7, grade 1
Brooker Creek Elementary School, Tarpon Springs, Florida (2012)

I don't always listen to brand music, with lyrics. Natural music also helps. I'll go to the pond, take the boat to the middle, and listen to the frogs, birds, and ducks sing their song. Music helps me find Radiant Peace.

~ Kristin, age 11, grade 5
Challenger 7 Elementary School, Cocoa, Florida (1998)

Sometimes I feel Radiant Peace when I am working in my garden. As I am hoeing it I look down and wonder what it's like to be a seed trying to break through the shell.

~ K.C., age 9, grade 3
Lancaster Elementary School, Lancaster, Kentucky (1998)

I help make more Radiant Peace in the world by growing a garden. The garden smells good and makes me feel peaceful. I share my food with my neighbors.

~ Emily Keehn, age 6, grade 1
St. Mark's Academy, Cocoa, Florida (2002)

Radiant Peace is a quiet feeling that starts in my heart and spreads all over me. Like when I am alone at the creek and everything is quiet. And when my kittens sit in my lap on a chilly day. And when I sit in the backyard and the wind rustles through the trees above me. And when the birds chirp as they fly above me. And when all is still and I lie in my bed and listen to the crickets outside. That's what Radiant Peace means to me.

~ Katelan Janke, age 8, grade 2
Hutto Elementary School, Hutto, Texas (1995)

I find Radiant Peace in myself by listening to nature. To me Radiant Peace means like going to outer space and listening to the beautiful sounds of comets shooting through the sky and shooting stars scooting through the universe....

~ Chris Duggan, age 8, grade 3
Academie Da Vinci, Dunedin, Florida (1999)

Radiant Peace is in people. Radiant Peace is in teachers and in all families. Radiant Peace is in plants. Radiant Peace is in the earth. It is in our dogs and cats and if you have a bird, it is in the bird too. Radiant Peace is in heaven and the most tiniest bug. That is what Radiant Peace is.

~ Hannah Cosner, age 7, grade 2
Pensacola Beach Elementary School, Pensacola Beach, Florida (1996)

Shh... sigh
Inhale, exhale
Listen
Silence, the kind that brings Radiant Peace
like the sun beating on my face,
the orange of the sunrise,
the kiss before bedtime.
Silence, the kind that brings Radiant Peace,
like the glow of a candle,
the leaves in a tree as the wind hits them,
the movement of the clouds across the sky.
Silence, the kind that brings Radiant Peace,
like the sound of waves hitting the shore,
the chirping of a cricket,
the light from fireflies on a dark night.
Shh... sigh
Inhale, exhale
Listen
Silence, the kind that brings Radiant Peace.

~ Christopher Barrocas, age 11, grade 6
St. Timothy Parish School, Miami, Florida (2011)

Radiant Peace is like the first spring bloom. Radiant Peace is like the sunrise. Radiant Peace is the happiness and joy that spreads through you to everyone.

~ Krishna Menon, age 9, grade 4
Ridgecrest Elementary School, Largo, Florida (2007)

I will share with you where I go to discover Radiant Peace in myself. I first go to the outside world and find a soft, comfy place in the grass. I hear the birds, watch the bees, and listen. I watch the lizards and look at flowers. I feel the heat of the sun on me. I take a deep breath and go inside... a brand new person. That is how I find Radiant Peace in myself.

~ Shaelyn Hayes, age 12, grade 6
Cape View Elementary School, Cape Canaveral, Florida (1998)

To me Radiant Peace is just sitting on my dock and watching a sun set, making the sky turn orange. This sight is a mind calming sight, it is just so relaxing. Another Radiant Peace moment to me is when my sister is playing with her dolls and I sit back from a distance and watch her. I think she displays a very good example of Radiant Peace every day.

~ Jake Trimble, age 11, grade 6
Westlake Christian School, Palm Harbor, Florida (2009)

Radiant Peace is the feeling you get when you lie on your back and watch the sunset. Radiant Peace is when you are on the beach very early, white sand under your feet, the gentle sound of waves lapping the shoreline. Nobody is around but you. Radiant Peace is when you are lying down beside a stream, listening to the water as it flows along its path.

~ Lucas Crawford, age 8, grade 3
Vance Elementary School, Vance, Alabama (2002)

Radiant Peace is walking through the forest, listening to a creek, and feeling the gentle breeze go by.

~ Jessica Dalton, age 10, grade 5
Crest Hill Elementary School, Casper, Wyoming (2008)

Radiant Peace is nature sounds. As the birds are chirping a song, and as the crickets are playing their violins, and as the trees are dancing with the wind, my heart fills with joy.

~ Makayla Rash, age 7, grade 2
Brooker Creek Elementary School, Tarpon Springs, Florida (2009)

Radiant Peace is as sweet as honey. It's within all human beings. It's the ingredient of kindness. Roses and dandelions sing Radiant Peace when you pick them. Radiant Peace is harmless to anyone or anything. Radiant Peace is as soft as a blanket. You can't feel it, but you know it's there. Radiant Peace means love and you can see it in the people you love most.

~ Xophye Coronel, age 8, grade 2
Walden Lake Elementary School, Plant City, Florida (2010)

Radiant Peace is sitting outside and listening to the birds sing. Radiant Peace is smelling the flowers on a sunny day.

~ Grizelle J. Kane, age 6, grade 1
Brooker Creek Elementary School, Tarpon Springs, Florida (2010)

Radiant Peace is like the wind in the trees, gradually migrating from one tree to another, making the leaves shift back and forth, back and forth.

~ Mindy D. Hitzel, age 10, grade 4
Perkins Elementary School, St. Petersburg, Florida (2006)

Radiant Peace is the breeze, flowing all around you. You don't see it; you feel it. It's a satisfying sensation that comes from deep within you. It warms you till everything in the world, everything around you is just a little brighter and all the more beautiful.

Radiant Peace is being satisfied with the life you've been given. It's looking at your family, your friends, every aspect and being thankful that you're alive, no matter what your circumstances. Radiant Peace is being happy standing in the sunshine and in the rain. Radiant Peace is taking a deep breath, taking a step forward, and just being yourself.

There is no one explanation or single statement that describes what Radiant Peace is to its full extent. Just like a breeze, it's constantly moving, changing and everyone feels it in their own way.

~ Alexandra Oliva, age 17, grade 11
Gibbs High School, St. Petersburg, Florida (2008)

Radiant Peace is like a flower, it starts out small then grows into something big and beautiful. Everyone has Radiant Peace inside them. Show Radiant Peace by being kind and respectful to others.

~ Emily Mueller, age 8, grade 3
Graebner Elementary School, Sterling Heights, Michigan (2007)

123

12 Radiant Peace on Earth, in the Solar System and in the Universe

Radiant Peace shines through you and touches everyone and everything in the universe.

~ Katie Brenner, age 13, grade 8
Unity School, Delray Beach, Florida (2011)

We should have pride for everyone in our hearts, for the earth, the water, and the life on the planet. Radiant Peace is like a song, a beautiful song, trying to be heard among us.

~ Leif Hoff-Holt, grade 5
Mayberry School, East Hartford, Connecticut (1991)

Most people's vision of Radiant Peace is limited only to the good of their country or state. Some consider the world. Very few think of how their thoughts or actions will affect other galaxies, or planets.... Just as Earth is not the only space with Radiant Peace, humans are not the only species who can feel it. Radiant Peace is capable of being absorbed by anything that lives, whether it is a rock or rabbit. Radiant Peace is everywhere.

~ Jessica Geragi, age 12, grade 7
Unity School, Delray Beach, Florida (2011)

I am a Radiant Peacemaker on earth when I share my kind heart when someone needs it. If everyone would do this the earth will be full of Radiant Peace!

~ Jin Sun Choi, grade 5
Anglo-American School of St. Petersburg, Russia (2008)

Radiant Peace is everywhere in our world.... There are millions of people who every year spend their time and money to help spread the word of peace throughout the world. But it's especially the little things such as a kiss on your mother's cheek in the morning, or a helping hand to a stranger that help spread it and change people's lives, incorporating Radiant Peace into everyone's day. This is what helps spread it throughout our world and through-out our solar system, and to an extent, the universe.

~ Aiden Lang, age 14, grade 8
Nuestro School, Live Oak, California (2009)

I am a Radiant Peacemaker when I do nice things for people and keep them in my thoughts. Also, by being a good friend, I can help people spread friendship, and find Radiant Peace in their hearts. I am a Radiant Peacemaker when I help those who are less fortunate than myself. I have talked, listened and even tap danced to make their hearts sing. Radiant Peace is "life" in ourselves. Let it flow from your heart. It is love, not hate. I can help people feel Radiant Peace from their head to their toes, and have it felt all over the universe. Let the light of Radiant Peace fill your heart and mind as it has mine. Remember, Radiant Peace is possible night and day.

~ Rebecca Elizabeth Wilson, age 10, grade 5
St. Mark's Academy, Cocoa, Florida (2000)

In my life, I learn from others. I have learned to be curious about other people. Radiant Peace in my life is the curiosity to explore other cultures. This inquisitive nature brings about understanding. Understanding the customs of someone else creates trust. This trust leads to acceptance, and for me, acceptance and inclusion of all people is Radiant Peace. Radiant Peace, however is more than the cooperation of human beings, but rather it is also the complete knowledge that there is more to a wheel than a single spoke, and so there is more to life than personal wants. We are all included in the universe, and we all have a reason to believe in Radiant Peace. Radiant Peace is something that you are born with the capability and desire to find, although I believe that it is through the search that we truly realize the meaning.

~ Samantha Grimes, age 13, grade 7
Largo Middle School, Largo, Florida (2010)

Radiant Peace is like having a star inside of us exuding light at all times. And when we do something kind, that star super-novas and it shines at its brightest.

~ Dylan Murphy, age 12, grade 6
St. Paul Catholic School, St. Petersburg, Florida (2011)

If I was an Emperor of the World, I would order Radiant Peace all over the Universe.

~ Bernadette Gulley, age 10, grade 5
Naranja Elementary School, Naranja, Florida (1992)

My most important way of finding Radiant Peace within is laying on a blanket on a clear night and looking at the stars with my Momma. I often wonder how far away they are.

~ Aaron Young, age 9, grade 4
Apollo Elementary School, Titusville, Florida (1999)

I'm not so sure I'm qualified to assess the status of Radiant Peace in the Universe, or the Solar System, to be completely honest. I've only ever been in one part out of the 28 billion light years (that's what's visible of the universe too) and I can truthfully say that my corner of the 28 billion confuses me more daily. It should also be noted that this is not my first attempt at this project. The first, a video, was abandoned due to my patience and artistic eye. Let it also be noted that, at this point in time, I have neither. Incidentally, I am sitting at my desk surrounded by books, letters, and a small but impressive collection of mini cacti, and I am officially starting over. First and foremost, what is Radiant Peace exactly? To me, it's a kind of inner balance between humility and humanity; a force, like a chi always pulling and pushing, keeping an absolute constant. But Radiant Peace means different things to all kinds of diverse people.

Sometimes I think about if there's life on other planets, and if these foreign life forms are like us, watching "Community" and arguing constantly about little slips of paper. Do they send their young off for 7+ hours a day to stare, and, occasionally, sleep in cold buildings that never, ever, have enough soap? And if there is life on other planets, why haven't they contacted us yet? Well, maybe they have. Maybe other life forms snuck in one day, dressed up like us and haven't left since. Maybe gradually, over months these newcomers developed Radiant Peace, the same way they learned how crosswalks work, and to avoid at all costs touching the handrails in a New York City subway. Or maybe they had it

(continued on next page)

(continued from previous page)

with them when they came, in suitcases of ribs, and coin purses filled with dust, and in fibers of beings. Maybe Radiant Peace isn't a uniquely Earthling trait, and we're all a little more alike than we may believe. A lot of maybes it seems like. It's probably safe to say, though, that these newbies talk about us behind our backs, maybe have their own exclusive social network where they post pictures of us being dumb and quote Snooki as if she's our supreme leader. Or maybe Snooki is one of them. Even better, maybe she's their supreme leader.

I don't know much about the universe and the solar system actually, and everything I do know was taught to me by Douglas Adams, but I think there is Radiant Peace out there. And I know it's here on earth. It ties us together on basic atomic levels; it's in the things we have in common; it's in laughter. It's on my school bus, and down my block, and you know, maybe it's even 28 billion light years away. But it's here; I see it every day.

~ Nell Clark, age 16, grade 10
Gibbs High School, St. Petersburg, Florida (2012)

Radiant Peace is like space. There are no obstacles in your way and it is endless.

~ Tyler Jackson, age 8, grade 2
Wellington School, St. Petersburg, Florida (2007)

Radiant Peace spreads from the crust of the Earth to space. In between all living things of Mother Earth are dancing, playing, laughing and no one is fighting.

~ Divya Arora, age 7, grade 1
Brooker Creek Elementary School, Tarpon Springs, Florida (2008)

Once upon a time there was a little princess. She waved her magic wand and wished for Radiant Peace in all the land. My magic wands are called Sharing and Caring and we can all spread Radiant Peace in the world by using them. Harmony can once again rule our wonderful world.

~ Andrea McCrary, age 7, grade 2
Lehigh Elementary School, Lehigh Acres, Florida (1996)

The purpose of this essay is to show how I can practice Radiant Peace. Until I heard about this contest I really never thought about what I can do as a ten-year-old child to promote Radiant Peace in the world. What can I do to help?

One thing I can do to help is to see what is going on in the world by watching the news, reading newspapers, books and looking at pictures.... I can start thinking about my role in daily life. How do I get along with my friends and family? Can the way I treat people and the way I am treated be a lesson on how to live a peaceful life?

How I feel is probably the key to my role in world Radiant Peace. Am I a good person? Am I fair with myself and others? I have a feeling this is the key to my role and my commitment.... After all, I guess I am thinking about the future of this planet.

~ Lauren Belle, age 10, grade 5
Parkview Elementary School, Baton Rouge, Louisiana (1991)

Radiant Peace is a peace that comes from your heart. It stays with you until you pass it on. Pass it on by simply smiling at someone. Do something nice and Radiant Peace travels. Do something extraordinary and it travels miles.

~ Ja'kaylah Danford, age 9, grade 4
Azalea Elementary School, St. Petersburg, Florida (2012)

Radiant Peace is what makes us whole and makes us who we are. Like love or joy; happiness. Everyone has it. It is the place inside of us that makes us feel at ease. Calm, like when we sleep. It lets us feel in tune with others, with nature, and the rest of the world. It helps us communicate and relate to others. In the universe, Radiant Peace is like the gravity that holds everything together. We need it....

~ Andrea Garaycoa, age 12, grade 7
St. Timothy Parish School, Miami, Florida (2009)

Radiant Peace can be shared with any living creature. Radiant Peace starts in your heart and spreads to your family then to your friends and then throughout the universe. I think Radiant Peace can live on for centuries if everyone cooperates.

~ Eric Yoshimura, grade 5
Turtleback Elementary School, San Diego, California (1991)

Radiant Peace is what you give not knowing who receives it.

~ Diego Orozco, age 9, grade 4
Ridgecrest Elementary School, Largo, Florida (2009)

Radiant Peace: most people think of mountains, or beaches, or sunrises, but I think of something much bigger, I think of the Universe. The way in perfect unity it is so large, so many planets, so many more stars. One of the most amazing things I can think of is how the remains of a supernova, the exploding death of a large star, can make another star, or even a planet. It is amazing that our Sun in our galaxy attracts the planets with its gravity. That the planets spin in a cosmic dance. That the Earth is the perfect distance from the sun to not burn us, but close enough to warm us. What may seem strange is that I find this peaceful, strangely calming; that it is in unison twirling around like dancers. Though it seems to some weird this is what I think is Radiant Peace, the humongous unity of it all.

~ Molly Brackett, age 14, grade 8
St. Paul Catholic School, St. Petersburg, Florida (2010)

Radiant Peace is shown throughout the universe, from the stars in the sky to the grass which we walk on. One must find this treasure within themselves. It is the key to survival for the whole human race.

~ Audrey M. Holloway, grade 8
Epiphany School, Normal, Illinois (1996)

The Radiant Peace Foundation International, Inc.

~ Committed to Radiant Peace ~

The Radiant Peace Foundation International is the only organization in the world dedicated to Radiant Peace. The Foundation is a 501(c)(3) educational nonprofit with headquarters in St. Petersburg, Florida.

The mission of The Radiant Peace Foundation International is:

- To inspire, encourage and promote Radiant Peace®
- To serve as a centerpoint for Radiant Peace education worldwide

Since its founding in 1986, The Radiant Peace Foundation International has offered educational programs and outreach around the world, including

- The Radiant Peace Education Awards®, offered every year since 1990
- The International Museum of Radiant Peace, established in 2001
- Celebrations of The International Day of Radiant Peace held worldwide since 1997
- Protection of special natural sites dedicated to Radiant Peace worldwide
- Recognition of outstanding Radiant Peacemakers
- Radiant Peace walks and events in many countries

The Radiant Peace Education Awards® — This program gives students in grades 1 - 12 the opportunity to submit essays, art and projects based on a Radiant Peace theme. Since 1990, more than 250,000 children have participated from throughout the United States. In addition, the program has expanded into twelve other countries on four continents. Senior citizens also participate in an awards program in which they reflect on Radiant Peace in their lives and in the world.

The International Museum of Radiant Peace — Established in 2001, this first-ever and only museum in the world dedicated to Radiant Peace is located in St. Petersburg, Florida. The museum features educational and interactive displays about Radiant Peace along with award-winning Radiant Peace essays, quotes, art and projects from adults and children around the world.

The International Day of Radiant Peace — Created in 1999, The International Day of Radiant Peace is celebrated every year on September 22 in schools, neighborhoods and cities in the United States and throughout the world. Commemorations of The International Day of Radiant Peace include city and state-wide proclamations recognizing The International Day of Radiant Peace, special Radiant Peace projects with children, ringing bells for Radiant Peace, and Radiant Peace picnics, walks and parties.

The educational programs and outreach of The Radiant Peace Foundation International are unique in the world. The Radiant Peace Foundation International is committed to Radiant Peace for all on this planet now and in future generations.

The Radiant Peace Education Awards®

Since 1990, The Radiant Peace Education Awards have reached hundreds of thousands of students across the United States, and, in recent years, in other countries. This educational program provides opportunities for people to learn about Radiant Peace® by writing essays or creating art and group projects. The Radiant Peace Education Awards have primarily been offered to students in grades 1 - 12. Senior citizens also participate in an awards program in which they reflect on Radiant Peace in their lives and in the world.

The Radiant Peace Education Awards are currently offered to students twice yearly, once in the fall and once in the spring. The program is available to students from public and private schools, home schools, and youth and after-school groups. Students write essays or create art, videos or projects about Radiant Peace. Every participant – students, teachers and staff – receives a beautiful iron-on Radiant Peace Patch. Outstanding entries also receive certificates and cash awards. In addition, many of the most creative or exceptional entries are displayed in The International Museum of Radiant Peace in St. Petersburg, Florida.

The Radiant Peace Education Awards give students the opportunity to express themselves about Radiant Peace. Teachers use the program within their class curriculum in a wide variety of ways to encourage literary and visual expression including developing and practicing writing skills, creative writing, artistic expression, and oral and visual communication. Entries can be submitted individually, as a group or classroom project, or as a multi-grade or whole-school project. The awards component of the program encourages participation and recognizes the participant's expression of Radiant Peace.

Thousands of entries to this program are received each year. The entries are evaluated by a team of teachers and other professionals using several criteria, including originality, sincerity, consistency of theme and overall composition. Winners are selected in several categories based on grade level and entry type. While the majority of entries are individual essays and art, the number of projects submitted continues to grow both in number and variety. Individual and group projects have included Radiant Peace songs, skits, public service announcements and video presentations of all kinds. Classroom and multi-grade projects include quilts (paper and cloth), banners, totem poles and shared writing projects – all with a Radiant Peace theme. One of the largest projects received was a "Wall of Radiant Peace," with each student creating a section.

Radiant Peace is inherently within all of us, yet people are not encouraged to learn about it. The Radiant Peace Education Awards program continues to offer this educational opportunity. Current information is available online at www.radiantpeace.org.

The International Museum of Radiant Peace

Established 2001

The International Museum of Radiant Peace, located in St. Petersburg, Florida, is the first-ever and only museum in the world dedicated to Radiant Peace®. Visitors to The International Museum of Radiant Peace learn about Radiant Peace through a wide variety of educational and interactive exhibits. This unique museum also showcases award-winning essays, quotes, art and projects about Radiant Peace from around the world.

The International Museum of Radiant Peace started in 2001 as a one-room exhibit of selected entries from the first eleven years of The Radiant Peace Education Awards® program. As larger and more varied entries were submitted, more rooms were added. In 2008, the space was remodeled and redesigned, officially becoming The International Museum of Radiant Peace. This first-ever museum dedicated to Radiant Peace welcomes visitors from around the world.

Museum exhibits change frequently to include current materials along with a selection of outstanding examples from the museum archives. The archives contain all the entries which have won awards in The Radiant Peace Education Awards program since 1990. Ongoing exhibits include "Radiant Peace and Animals," "Radiant Peace in the Solar System" and "Radiant Peace around the World." Museum educators provide tours and also offer community outreach programs for local schools and civic organizations.

Many visitors to The International Museum of Radiant Peace have commented that this special place offers inspiration and renewal in an often challenging and stressful world. The Museum is a not-to-be-missed attraction in the Tampa Bay area!

Frequently Asked Questions

What is Radiant Peace®?

Radiant Peace is natural, whole, harmless, benevolent energy within all our hearts relating us all and making us whole. Radiant Peace is not dualistic in nature, as in cycles of war and peace. Radiant Peace transcends the limits of race, age, gender, politics and religion.

What is the mission of The Radiant Peace Foundation International?

★ to inspire, encourage and promote Radiant Peace®
★ to serve as a centerpoint for Radiant Peace education worldwide

How can I get information about The Radiant Peace Education Awards®?

The current announcement, including guidelines, permission forms and deadlines, is available on the Foundation Web site at radiantpeace.org. The Radiant Peace Education Awards are offered twice yearly, once in the fall and once in the spring. If you would like to receive an announcement by mail, contact the Foundation office.

Who can participate in The Radiant Peace Education Awards®?

The Radiant Peace Education Awards are open to all students in grades 1-12 from public and private schools, home schools, youth and after-school groups, and abroad. Every participant receives a Radiant Peace Patch, and outstanding entries also receive cash awards and certificates.

How is The Radiant Peace Foundation International funded?

The Radiant Peace Foundation International and all Radiant Peace programs and outreach are funded by donations from individuals and corporations.

Are there Radiant Peace activities in my area?

There can be! Just decide what you would you like to do to inspire, encourage and promote Radiant Peace. Radiant Peace activities can take place in neighborhoods, workplaces, schools and communities. Many ideas are available on the Foundation Web site (radiantpeace.org). Materials such as the Radiant Peace banner and Radiant Peace Patches are available for activities upon request.

What is The International Day of Radiant Peace?

The International Day of Radiant Peace is celebrated every year on September 22 in schools and communities in the United States and throughout Europe, Australia, Asia and South America. This special day was created in 1999 as a day for people to remember, celebrate and commemorate Radiant Peace wherever they are. Commemorations of The International Day of Radiant Peace include city and state-wide proclamations recognizing The International Day of Radiant Peace, special Radiant Peace projects with children, ringing bells for Radiant Peace, and Radiant Peace picnics and parties.

"I love what that child wrote. I want to use it on my Web site/ in my office/on a card...."

All content in this book is protected under copyright and may not be reproduced or distributed without written permission.

Why do you have the ® after Radiant Peace®?

Radiant Peace® is a service mark (trademark) registered and held by The Radiant Peace Foundation International, Inc. The owner of this service mark is the only entity permitted to use this mark commercially, just as with trademarks such as Coca-Cola® or Apple®. The Foundation must grant prior written permission to anyone else using this service mark.

How do I contact The Radiant Peace Foundation International?

Mail:

The Radiant Peace Foundation International, Inc.
P.O. Box 40822
St. Petersburg, FL 33743

Email: RadiantPeaceIntl@gmail.com

Web: www.radiantpeace.org

Phone: 727-343-8212

How can I help?

The Radiant Peace Foundation International, Inc. is a 501(c)(3) educational nonprofit and relies solely on contributions. Every donation helps to continue programs and outreach which are essential to Radiant Peace education worldwide.

Purposes of
The Radiant Peace
Foundation International, Inc.

1. To inspire, encourage and promote Radiant Peace®, which is natural, whole, harmless, not dualistic, benevolent energy within all our hearts relating us all and making us whole. Radiant Peace transcends the limits of race, age, gender, politics and religion. Radiant Peace is within us all and is available to everyone;

2. To contribute to increasing the knowledge and understanding of Radiant Peace, as it recognizes the dignity and worth of all human beings, of all animals and of all living things, and to promote right human relations and peaceful co-existence among all peoples and all living things on earth in Radiant Peace;

3. To support increased understanding of Radiant Peace, honoring the peaceful inter-connectedness of all life, and the essential oneness of all life;

4. To develop through education, research and distribution of materials widespread understanding of Radiant Peace which is naturally nurturing, beneficial and benevolent to all peoples and aligned with the basic human right to achieve wholeness, balance, health in body, mind and spirit, integrity, intelligence, and love;

5. To promote international understanding and cooperation in responsible service for human, and all life, in mutual respect, love and harmlessness, in peaceful caretaking and in the inclusive principle of unity within our diversities, which is Radiant Peace;

6. To be a centerpoint for and to cooperate with other organizations in activities and education contributing to Radiant Peace, global stability, unity, and the continuing development of right human relations;

7. To celebrate The International Day of Radiant Peace and The International Festival of Radiant Peace each year, and to inspire, encourage and promote Radiant Peace worldwide.

How You Can Help

Please donate to support Radiant Peace programs! Every donation helps to continue the programs and outreach which are essential to Radiant Peace education worldwide.

Donate securely online at

www.radiantpeace.org

via Paypal to

RadiantPeaceIntl@gmail.com

or mail your donation to

The Radiant Peace Foundation International, Inc.
P.O. Box 40822
St. Petersburg FL 33743

Thank you!

www.ingramcontent.com/pod-product-compliance
Lightning Source LLC
Chambersburg PA
CBHW071958170626
46813CB00005B/1915